# DEALING WITH THE UNAVOIDABLE NARCISSIST IN YOUR LIFE

## A STRATEGIC BLUEPRINT FOR COPING WITH DIFFICULT RELATIONSHIPS

SYDNEY KOH

*To those who find strength and courage*

*each day to rebuild themselves*

*despite being torn down by a narcissist.*

*May you find your voice and regain your sense of self.*

# CONTENTS

**A Free Gift for our Readers**

Did you just discover the difficult relationship in your life is with a narcissist?

I polled thousands of survivors and asked one question: What were the most impactful first steps you took in your narcissistic abuse recovery?

This is what they told me.

Download your free guide below!

*Your 7 Step Journey to Narcissistic Abuse Recovery*

*www.TrilliumSage.com*

# INTRODUCTION

Nothing is more harrowing than the emptiness in the pit of despair that we feel growing deeper and deeper in our hearts. Nothing is more challenging than being faced with a narcissist who refuses to acknowledge our suffering and trauma—all the while blaming us for our misery. At first, we blame ourselves for failing to please our narcissists, for failing to recognize their many favors, and for cherishing their grander-than-grand presence in our lives. If only we hadn't spoken too loudly or given in to their multitude of demands, we could have prevented them from losing their cool and shouting at us with rage in their eyes. Perhaps, if we had been more meticulous in executing their commands with the perfection they demand of us, we could have secured their love. The struggle always seemed never-ending, and we were constantly bending over backward, trying to appease them and win over their approval and love, but . . . we could never be enough.

Sounds familiar, doesn't it? It's the story of every person who has lived with and survived the abuse of a narcissist. For some, the narcissists in their lives are their parents, who are supposed to be selfless and compassionate caregivers. Others struggle with narcissistic siblings, bosses, coworkers, in-laws, ex-spouses, or friends. In my story, the narcissist was my husband, the father of my three beautiful sons, and a man I desperately tried to love with all my heart.

I am Sydney Koh, a doting mother to three teenage sons and a German Shepherd, a passionate traveler, wine enthusiast, and homemaker. I was married to my narcissist husband for a long and exhausting period of 15 years. It took years of trauma, exploitation, manipulation, abuse, and struggle for me to finally give up and walk out with my children and self-esteem. In my quest to reclaim my identity and power, I decided to end the trauma, and just two weeks before we finalized our divorce, my narcissist husband took his own life.

My agonizing journey of 15 years of enduring the pain, suffering, and psychological abuse of being married to a narcissist does not make me an expert on narcissistic personality disorder (NPD). However, my quest for a healthy, fulfilling, and rewarding life for myself and my children motivated me to seek the education necessary for empowerment. I wish to share this power with you. I am far too familiar with the trauma of not understanding what's wrong and how much of it is your fault because a narcissist will always twist words around and gaslight you into believing you're the culprit.

I remember how empowering it felt when I first reached out for support in my Facebook support group. The experiences I came across reaffirmed my faith in my intuition: I was not the problem. I did not cause this mess. I want to share some of the excerpts from these experiences with you, so you know that you're not alone, you're not imagining things, and no one has the right to attack your self-esteem and trample over your emotions. Take a quick look at the following firsthand accounts from survivors of my Facebook group. I imagine these quotes will stir deep emotions within you as you find strikingly familiar struggles in your own experience. Please note that all contributor names referenced below have been altered to protect the privacy of the survivors.

*"Seeking external validation is their game, but it also takes a lot of energy for them to fake their persona, so they release aggression on their victim behind closed doors."*

— MORGAN, ON RECEIVING ABUSE IN
PRIVATE

*"Their biggest concern/fear is being exposed for who and what they really are, so they will smear your name to give them a head start in any exposure plans."*

— JULIA, ON HER NARCISSIST'S SMEAR
CAMPAIGN

*". . . Mine went over to my mom's and her husband's without me, and I don't know what he said, but when he discarded me, they took him in and aren't talking to me anymore. [My husband and I] had a very good and close relationship with my mom, and [my mom and me], before that. It breaks my heart to lose the biggest supporter in my life I ever had."*

— PATRICIA, ON HER STRUGGLES WITH A
NARCISSISTIC HUSBAND

*"My ex still fools people today, including his family. They even somehow believe when he punched me, it was my fault. I left after the physical abuse started."*

— NATASHA, ON PHYSICAL ABUSE

*"Mine was a distinguished gentleman from the UK who holds a high position at our workplace. He appears to be very charming and a friend to all. That's how he sucked me in. If they only knew what a monster he really is. If you're not a victim, you could never understand. I left my job recently to escape from the constant hoovers. I wonder what he's telling people now. I'm sure it's all great things. You know how they twist reality and make us look like the evil ones. Psychopaths. The person I know and the person they know are two entirely different people.*

*When people tell me how nice he is, it makes me physically ill. If only they knew the mental anguish he put me through. He's an actor, and he plays his parts well."*

— ABBY, ON DEALING WITH A NARCISSIST
IN THE WORKPLACE

I decided to write this book after being empowered by the experiences of others and to bring awareness to help victims actualize their power. Narcissistic abuse is not a typical form of abuse, so having support from people who have experienced this specific type of abuse is priceless. The support and clarity I received by understanding that I'm not alone in this struggle helped me enormously, showing me that there is a way out for my children and me. I want to share this empowerment with all those who feel hopeless, helpless, and don't understand how to fight back. Once you are familiar with the traits and complexities of a narcissist, you will find it easier to channel the power you need to reclaim your life. Understanding a narcissist's mind and employing the strategies we will be discussing will strengthen you to take action and protect yourself.

*"Nobody can be kinder than the narcissist while you react to life on his terms."*

— ELIZABETH BOWEN

# PART I

UNDERSTANDING NARCISSISM

# 1

# ARE NARCISSISTS EVIL?

L ove is as delicate as it is fierce, and the human psychology of reciprocation is what makes our relationships stronger and lasting. When we love someone unconditionally—be it our parents, siblings, spouses, romantic partners, or children—our love gives birth to a million conscious and unconscious expectations. And when we realize that we will always find ourselves on the giving end of a relationship, this realization shatters our hearts and self-esteem. When we are hurt, disappointed and angry, demonizing the culprit behind such negativity is the only logical solution, right? Except that it isn't, because that's just an easy way out. Understanding the underlying problems behind narcissistic behavior is a harrowing and exhaustive struggle that requires us to peel away all the exterior layers and get to the bottom of a complex personality disorder.

This book will not encourage you to demonize people or blame them for their selfish behaviors, even though blaming and demonizing may give you some semblance of closure and clarity. Shifting the blame will not help you break free from this vicious cycle and put an end to generational patterns of abuse and emotional trauma. So, what will help?

Understanding narcissistic personalities and realizing that a mental health illness is at play here will prove monumentally helpful in mending your relationships and actualizing your strength and confidence while dealing with narcissistic personalities. It is imperative that our mindset shifts from simply labeling the narcissist as evil to understanding their behavior. Doing so is critical in transforming the abused from victim to survivor. Of course, this is not to say that the deeds and actions of a narcissist are *not* evil, but perhaps the effects stem from a personality disorder, and we should at least take the time to understand what we might be dealing with.

In this chapter, we will discuss all the complexities and dynamics of narcissistic personality disorder (NPD) and offer you a glimpse into the mind of a narcissist. But as I walk you through these eye-opening details, I urge you to keep an open mind and read with compassion because a mental illness brings suffering for everyone, the sufferers, and whoever they hold dear in life.

## THE COMPLEX MIND OF A NARCISSIST

What does the term narcissism signify? It refers to someone who appears to be obsessed with themselves and excessively vain over their beauty, success, riches, or other bounties. We are all familiar with the intriguing tale of the Greek god Narcissus, who fell in love with his great beauty after seeing his reflection in a pool of water and ended up spending his entire life staring at his reflection.

Interestingly, the psychological definition of narcissism is strikingly different from the notions of vanity and pride that we commonly associate with the term. The study of human psychology reveals that narcissism is much more complex than just self-love or vanity because it is a mindset that thrives on delusions and illusions. People with NPD have an idealized and grander-than-grand view of themselves, and they sustain this image of grandeur by feeding their vanity and self-esteem at the expense of others.

Narcissistic personality disorder is characterized as a continuing pattern of mental, emotional, and behavioral experiences dominated by an exaggerated sense of self-significance, self-centered behaviors, lack of empathy and concern for others, and a lofty image of self (Cherry, 2020). This disorder is one of the many personality disorders classified in the Diagnostic and Statistical Manual of Mental Disorders (DSM-5), a set pattern of criteria practitioners consult before diagnosing someone with this or any other personality disorder.

Narcissistic personality disorder brings about disruptive pathological personality traits that stem from functional impairments. Like other personality disorders, NPD negatively impacts a person's family life, social circle, and work-related relationships.

Let's take a look at the symptoms of this disorder (Cherry, 2020):

- An exaggerated sense of self-importance.
- A strong sense of being special and unique.
- Creating a lofty status for self, and a desire to associate with people who enjoy the same grand status.
- Constantly craving praise, applause, attention, and affirmations.
- An exaggerated sense of one's accomplishments, qualities, and abilities.
- Willingness to exploit others for vested interests and gains.
- Lack of empathy and compassion towards the plight of others.
- Feelings of competitiveness and envy towards others.
- Constantly believing that others are envious and jealous of them.
- Stubborn fantasies and ideals of achieving great power and success.
- An obsession with success and power.

- A strong sense of entitlement and demanding to be treated with exclusivity and splendor.
- Expecting special treatment from all those close to them.

People with NPD are often criticized for being self-centered, proud, arrogant, smug, and self-important. These beliefs stem from their self-image and aggressively competitive and envious streaks. They expect to be treated like a celebrity, commanding unconditional love and respect, despite their lack of empathy towards the sufferings of others. Naturally, they regard themselves as superior beings and stubbornly hoard and accumulate things and luxuries that sustain their image of leading a prosperous and abundant lifestyle. It may come as a surprise, but this grand and lofty self-image actually stems from the abundance of insecurities that narcissists keep bottled within themselves.

Their insecurities always get the best of them, despite their exaggerated sense of self and the grandiosity they associate with their personality traits and abilities. These insecurities make them increasingly reliant on applause and affirmations, and they want their family and friends to shower them with constant praise and attention. Why is that? Because constant attention and applause are crucial to sustain their self-image and strengthen their self-esteem. They thrive on the adoration, admiration, and continuous validation they demand from their victims. This validation is the "supply" that feeds them. If you live or work with a narcissist, you must have noticed how vulnerable they are to criticism and how furiously they detest any kind of disapproval. People with narcissistic personality disorder regard criticism, even if it is constructive and well-intended, as a personal attack against their glory and magnificence.

People with NPD exhibit exalting confidence, and one is compelled to believe that the sun shines and sets on their face. Their extroverted charm and flamboyant nature are very appealing. However, when you get closer, you find yourself dealing with a personality that is constantly craving and consuming attention with no intention to spare a few minutes to empathize with others. These people wear an intricately woven façade of self-assurance, poise, and confidence. When this façade is peeled off, what lies beneath the surface are vulnerabilities and insecurities. These people are increasingly vulnerable, and their self-esteem is shrouded in deep-rooted insecurities, pushing them to constantly obtain validation and praise from others.

## WHAT IS NPD? UNDERSTANDING ITS PATHOLOGICAL PERSONALITY TRAITS & SIGNS

We all exhibit the occasional streak of self-absorption, self-centeredness, and selfishness that make us blind to the needs of others, encouraging us to focus solely on our own desires and needs. Narcissism is a common behavioral trait found in almost all humans, but does that mean everyone is at risk for developing narcissistic personality disorder? That's not quite how it works, and it's crucial to avoid labeling our loved ones with stigmas and psychological terms that do not reflect their behaviors. The Diagnostic and Statistical Manual of Mental Disorders (DSM) was introduced for this reason: to establish scientific rules and processes to categorize mental disorders and psychological conditions with appropriate diagnostic procedures.

How is someone diagnosed with a personality disorder as complex and multifaceted as narcissistic personality disorder? Consistency is of the utmost significance here, as the patient must exhibit certain pathological traits and narcissistic behaviors for a prolonged period. Experts from the American Psychiatric Association reveal that a personality disorder interferes with a person's thought patterns and behaviors, altering the way they think, empathize, relate, and connect with others (Kritz, 2020). Essentially, a personality disorder manifests itself in the form of "impairments in personality." So, when does narcissism, a personality trait, develop into a full-blown personality disorder?

We must refer back to the mythical tale of the Greek god Narcissus, who fell in love with the image of his youthful beauty and spent the rest of his life staring at that image and marveling at his gorgeousness. What does this story reveal? It reveals a consistent pattern of narcissistic behaviors and personality traits.

We all exhibit narcissistic traits and make selfish choices every now and then. There's absolutely nothing wrong with deciding to put yourself first and respecting your desires over the desires, expectations, and demands others make of you. So, when does narcissism become a personality disorder? According to the DSM criteria, when it starts interfering with an individual's ability to function as a constructive and responsible person who engages mindfully and respectfully with others.

Research-driven insights from the Mayo Clinic (Kritz, 2020) offer a clinical glance into people's personality traits and behaviors with NPD. As discussed earlier, they radiate with shining confidence that attracts people towards them like moths buzzing around a flame. They enjoy holding court and enthralling a captivated audience with tales of their grandeur, bravado, and other exceptional qualities and adventurous escapades. They like coming out as the knight in shining armor in every story they share. Still, once you explore beneath the surface, you see an insecure and vulnerable personality that craves attention and applause to bolster their self-esteem. Their stubborn disregard for the feelings and emotional boundaries of others is another prominent personality trait. People with NPD exhibit little or no empathy for others. They wear a façade of self-assurance and poise, but inwardly, they struggle with vulnerabilities that gnaw at their self-esteem, compelling them to seek approval. These individuals constantly need validation, and a failure to obtain this much-needed approval results in a deep depression and a throbbing sense of inadequacy. These traits combine to create a personality that struggles to form and maintain lasting relationships based on mutual care, respect, and trust. In simpler terms, NPD is the clinical form of persistent narcissistic behavior that gives rise to emotional distress, impaired functioning, and fractured relationships.

Behavioral psychologists reveal that people diagnosed with NPD exhibit a series of personality traits to establish their superiority over others (Kacel et al., 2017).

**These traits include the following:**

- An inability to take criticism constructively.
- Associating great significance and importance with themselves.
- An inflated sense of their ability to succeed and hold great power.
- A constant need for admiration, applause, and approval.

So you see, the problem takes root when a person's notions of grandeur and self-importance overshadow their ability to nurture and empathize with others, disrupting their personal and professional lives drastically. Experts reveal two different kinds of narcissism (Brazier, 2020):

1. Grandiose Narcissism
2. Vulnerable Narcissism

What makes these two different? As the word implies, grandiose is synonymous with an overwhelming sense of entitlement, flashy and bold claims of superiority, and ostentatious behavior. On the other hand, vulnerable narcissism reflects a hypersensitivity that stems from deep-rooted introversion and insecurities. Both these forms are grounded in profoundly self-absorbed and selfish behaviors and an inability to empathize with others.

We brushed over the symptoms of NPD earlier, but now, we'll take a closer look at the pathological traits associated with this condition. It is pertinent to note that not all people diagnosed with NPD manifest the same characteristics and symptoms (Kritz, 2020).

**Arrogance & Boastfulness**

Aside from their entitlement and self-importance, arrogance is a dominant trait that makes them appear overly pretentious. The narcissists' willingness and joy to boast their own praises reflect an exaggerated sense of their accomplishments and abilities. These people seem obsessed with fantasizing about amassing a great fortune, enjoying unparalleled success, possessing unrivaled beauty, or rising to enormous power. A person who is well-grounded and humble can feel incredibly uncomfortable and belittled in their presence.

## Sense of Superiority

Their overpowering and robust sense of superiority encourages them to build relationships with people they regard as equals in accomplishments, success, intellect, power, wealth, or beauty. They seldom allow others to speak up and end up monopolizing the entire conversation, making the other person feel helpless and unable to express themselves. Their haughty demeanor and sense of superiority encourage them to belittle people actively and look down on their disadvantages and problems. They are known to be highly manipulative and tend to benefit at the expense of others.

## Inability to Empathize

When do these traits start interfering with their relationships with parents, siblings, spouses, children, and friends? This occurs when they begin exhibiting an acute inability and a stubborn unwillingness to accept and respect the feelings, needs, and desires of others. Narcissists are entirely oblivious to the feelings and emotions of others, but what's even more surprising is their inability to understand how feelings and emotions work.

It's normal for narcs to blame others for how they feel. Whether their feelings are positive or negative, they don't realize their own role in their thoughts and cognitive patterns. They are blind to their feelings and blame others for making them feel the way they do, which makes them utterly blind to the feelings of others. Expecting a narcissist to understand your pain and suffering is more futile than expecting a concrete wall to move.

## Jealousy

Jealousy is another dominant personality trait that manifests itself in the form of a fierce competitive streak. People with NPD tend to envy others, and they also nurture beliefs that others are jealous of them and secretly plotting their demise.

## Nothing but the Best

Here's another manifestation of their competitive streak: they desire nothing but the best. Be it clothing, property, wealth, career-related success, or domestic life—narcissists want nothing but the best. Anything they deem less than the best holds little or no significance in their minds and often ends up distancing and alienating their loved ones and close family members.

## Difficulties Accepting Criticism

People with NPD have an incredibly tough time embracing criticism and using it constructively to reflect inwardly and make amends. Naturally, this creates an abundance of challenges and conflicts in their personal and professional relationships. This inability to accept criticism impairs their ability to connect and form relationships.

## Anger & Impatience

People often end up feeling like it's now or never when dealing with narcissists. They find themselves pitted against a personality that is impatient and nearly impossible to please. People with NPD expect special treatment, and they will not hold back their anger and fury when denied the special treatment they so aggressively demand. Family members and loved ones often feel like they're walking on eggshells, struggling to please a narcissist who is likely to feel affronted at the slightest error. The stress and anxiety stemming from such a relationship are often too much to bear, and narcissists often react with unrestrained rage to bolster their superiority. This rage can leave the other person feeling unfairly targeted with contempt as they did nothing to deserve this treatment, making them feel helpless and belittled.

## Emotional Difficulties

So far, we've been talking about the negative traits that give rise to toxic patterns that create distress for others, allowing the narcissist to revel in their perceived glory. But here's a pathological characteristic that helps us understand people's emotional turmoil and vulnerabilities with NPD.

These people have acute difficulty regulating their behaviors and emotions. They struggle to process emotions and deal with stress of any kind. Embracing and adapting to change requires a Herculean effort on their part. These emotional disturbances stem from underlying seeds:

vulnerabilities, insecurities, a deep-rooted sense of shame, and the perpetual fear of humiliation.

## UNRAVELING THE CAUSES OF NARCISSISM

Research from The National Institute of Mental Health Information Resource Center (n.d.) reveals that around 9.1% of American adults are at risk of developing at least one kind of personality disorder. Over the years, statistical revelations suggest that just over 6% of adults in the US have specifically been diagnosed with a narcissistic personality disorder. Insight from The Journal of Clinical Psychiatry (Stinson et al., 2008) suggests that men have a greater risk for NPD, with a chance of 7.7%, while women have a risk of 4.8%.

Interestingly, clinical experts suggest that NPD is more closely linked with mental disabilities and disturbances in men than women (Stinson et al., 2008). Experts have also observed the consistent occurrence of overlapping symptoms alongside NPD traits (Brazier, 2020).

These co-occurring mental disabilities include:

- Substance abuse
- Anxiety disorders
- Mood disorders
- Bipolar disorder
- Specific phobias
- Post-traumatic stress disorder

Processing these clinical observations can prove over-whelming, so let's answer a more straightforward question: what causes a person to develop a personality disorder like NPD? Naturally, the answer to such a multifaceted question is anything but simple, but we'll try to focus on the issues in a relatable manner. Research suggests that childhood experiences, parenting style, and upbringing are crucial factors in the causes behind NPD (Kritz, 2020). However, genetics is another likely factor that's gaining traction in recent debates (Mitra & Fluyau, 2021).

**Environmental Factors**

Our environment is a significant contributor to our personality traits and behaviors. Our relationship with our culture and our parents is an essential factor contributing to the development of NPD. It appears that individualistic cultures that promote the goals, rights, and ambitions of an individual tend to encourage narcissistic behaviors. In contrast, collectivist cultures, which promote mutual success and goals, are less likely to promote narcissism.

**Childhood Experiences & Parenting Styles**

Childhood experiences have a crucial role to play in the risk factors of NPD. Adverse childhood experiences, such as being shunned by a parent or overly criticized, are likely to lead to adult NPD development. Surprisingly, the same results also hold in parents who shower their children with undue praise.

Much has been written and said about parenting styles and the development of NPD. There's no concrete research that nails down specific parenting styles that develop narcissistic traits in young adults. And yet, research suggests a link between parenting styles and the disorder (Brazier, 2020).

Here are some parenting styles that are associated with narcissistic traits in children:

- Helicopter parenting, i.e., being overprotective and coddling.
- Being overly lenient with little or no restrictions.
- An inability to express warmth to one's child.
- Exaggerated praise that gives rise to unrealistic notions of perfection and grandeur.
- Abusive and disrespectful.
- Maltreatment.

Interestingly, overprotection and helicopter parenting are associated with both grandiose and vulnerable narcissism. It comes as no surprise that excessive and undue praise is associated with illusions of superiority and grandeur. A failure to set appropriate boundaries and disciplining restrictions were found related to vulnerable narcissism.

**Genetic Factors**

Recent clinical findings reveal that genetics have a prominent role in developing narcissistic personality disorder. A behavioral study investigated patterns of NPD traits in

304 pairs of twins. This study revealed a hereditary rate of 23% for grandiosity and 35% for entitlement (Luo et al., 2014).

**Personality Traits**

Our personality traits also come into play in a disorder as complex and multifaceted as NPD. People who have a strong sense of entitlement, dominating behaviors, and heightened focus on themselves are more likely to develop grandiose narcissism. Vulnerable narcissism is closely tied with self-focused introversion, aggressive mood swings, a deep-rooted sense of shame, and bouts of pride and boastfulness.

## TREATING NARCISSISTIC PERSONALITY DISORDER: THERAPY, MEDICATIONS & MORE

There are various treatment options and therapies available with the remarkable potential to help people with NPD combat their condition with mindful strategies and powerful skills. Essentially, these skills and strategies serve the purpose of assisting them to connect, empathize and relate with others. These techniques and practices are designed to help people with NPD channel a positive change in their personalities to reflect improvement and enrichment in their personal and work relationships.

However, the success of any treatment, be it therapy or medications, is met with an enormous challenge. Most people with a personality disorder, especially narcissistic personality disorder, do not seek treatment because they don't believe there's something wrong with their behavior or personality. In most cases, these people only consider therapy or mental health advice or intervention when their behaviors disrupt other aspects of their lives and careers.

As discussed earlier, people with NPD are also at a higher risk of struggling from a vast host of mental health conditions. Prevalently, these conditions are depression, substance abuse or alcohol dependence, and anxiety disorder. In most cases, people seek mental health professionals to treat their anxiety, depression, or substance dependence rather than NPD. As a rule, people with NPD only seek treatment after their family and loved ones stage an intervention, forcing them to believe their behavior is unhealthy.

When people with NPD willingly seek treatment, it's not because they believe their personality traits are toxic or unhealthy. They seek treatment to deal with their emotional conflicts and disturbances. For instance, they seek therapy to overcome the stress of outcomes and relationships that don't satisfy their high and mighty standards. Or when they have to struggle to capture someone's interest or attention. Seeking treatment or coming to terms with their unhealthy traits is not easy for a person with NPD. Even when they start therapy, they struggle to understand that the emotional disturbances they are experiencing stem from their personality traits. These people are more likely to blame others for their negative emotions. Instead of transforming their unhealthy patterns, they often regard therapy as an outlet to pin the blame on others, vent out their frustration, deny responsibility, and seek sympathy for their self-perceived disadvantages.

A lasting commitment to treatment is another struggle that denies people with NPD the necessary transformation to improve their lives and connect with their loved ones. People with NPD struggle to stay in therapy long enough to make a transformative impact that can result in long-term changes in their personality and behavioral traits. It's imperative to understand that these people struggle with communication and interactions. When they find themselves in a therapist-client setting, it's not easy for them to peel away those layers and reveal their vulnerabilities. Instead, they are likely to build a dramatic façade of self-assuredness and poise since they are increasingly aware of the therapist's calculated posture and diligent note-taking movements.

Essentially, the treatment challenges culminate in their inability and unwillingness to realize their personality and behavior are the root cause of the problem. When a person with NPD decides to continue therapy, they are likely to exhibit little or no progress because they are reluctant to embrace any kind of change—a core personality trait. Their unwillingness and inability to accept responsibility for their actions is another prominent trait that prevents them from realizing the need to transform their behavior and make amends. The way they see it;

there's no valid reason for them to change as both their behavior and personality are the epitome of perfection. Convincing a person with such a mindset to embrace change is often seen as a gross insult to their grandeur.

**Psychotherapy**

Psychotherapy as a long-term treatment has proven immensely effective in helping people overcome the toxic personality traits associated with NPD (Cherry, 2021a). Various psychotherapy techniques help treat people with NPD.

The most effective psychotherapy approaches include:

- Cognitive behavioral therapy (CBT)
- Psychoanalytic therapy
- Metacognitive interpersonal therapy
- Schema-focused psychotherapy
- Dialectical behavior therapy
- Individual psychodynamic psychotherapy

All the above-mentioned therapies revolve around one basic premise: helping people understand their behaviors, achieving a more realistic sense of self, and eliminating their unhealthy behaviors by realizing their negative impacts. Cognitive behavioral therapy (CBT) is one of the most effective techniques to help people with NPD understand the destructive effects of their personality traits, thought processes, and behaviors. CBT aims to help people rationalize their distorted versions of reality to establish a realistic understanding of themselves (Cherry, 2021a).

It is common for clinical psychologists to combine therapy with psychotropic medications to help people with NPD manage overlapping symptoms of anxiety, depression, and mood imbalances. Medications help these people commit to long-term treatment and stay consistent in channeling the change they need to transform their lives and relationships (Salters-Pedneault, 2020).

How can therapy help a person who commits to a long-term course of treatment with a dedicated therapist?

Long-term therapy helps people with NPD in the following ways (Cherry, 2021a):

- Understanding and processing complex emotions.
- Realizing attitudes, mindsets, behaviors, and traits that promote conflicts with others.
- Identifying strategies to overcome toxic behaviors and prevent unhealthy patterns.
- Developing skills to empathize, connect and relate with others.
- Learn techniques to foster reliable, stable, and intimate connections.
- Learning to embrace criticism and use feedback constructively.
- Identifying coping mechanisms to combat stress, anxiety, and depression.

- Understanding deep-rooted insecurities that give rise to narcissistic behaviors.
- Developing a mindset that is tolerant, accepting, and encouraging of the opinions of others.

Each person struggling with NPD has a different journey and an entirely different set of struggles. There is no one-size-fits-all solution when it comes to treating NPD. All humans are different and unique, and naturally, therapies and treatments are tailored to address the needs and requirements of the individual person. Understanding such a complex disorder that reinforces illusions of superiority and perfection is never easy because people with NPD have blind confidence in their faultlessness. Though it is near impossible to cure a person of NPD, long-term therapy and treatment can help them overcome negative behaviors and bring about positive change in their lives.

## BUSTING COMMON NPD MYTHS & MISCONCEPTIONS

If you're living with a narcissist or managed to break free from a toxic relationship with one, it's hard to stop yourself from demonizing them and painting them as the villain. It will take every ounce of your willpower and inner strength to look past the emotional trauma, discomfort, and suffering they've caused you and make an attempt to understand the reasons behind their toxic traits. Very few manage to make this effort because most people have struggled with emotional disturbances, stress, and trauma resulting from their experiences with narcissists. I do not consider myself an authority, but as someone who has loved, lived with, and raised a family with a narcissist. I want to urge you to rid of all the myths and misconceptions that keep us from peeling away those layers that shroud the vulnerabilities of people with NPD.

Here are some common myths and misconceptions we need to dispel before diving deeper into this book (Greenberg, 2021):

- Narcissists are peace-sucking vampires who prey on the vulnerabilities and emotions of people who care about others.
- Narcissists are inherently evil, with the devil permanently seated on their left shoulder.
- All narcissists are the same, with little hope of ever realizing their toxic traits.
- People are 100% in control of their narcissistic behaviors.
- Narcissists cannot cultivate intimate relationships.
- Narcissists can never change their selfish traits.
- Narcissists received excessive praise and attention from their parents.
- Narcissists are constantly oozing out charm and charisma.
- Narcissists intentionally plot to hurt and manipulate their loved ones.

- Narcissists are sexually promiscuous and indulgent.
- Manipulation is an inherent trait in narcissists.
- Narcissists are inherently evil beings.

Reading through these toxic phrases and sentences makes us realize the problem with these myths: they make us think much like a person with NPD. Such myths and misconceptions blind us to the suffering of a person struggling to cope with the overwhelming emotional disturbances triggered by overlapping mental disorders. Demonizing a narcissist and regarding them as evil blood-sucking hounds will not serve a constructive purpose. Understanding the dynamics of the illness and refusing to demonize our narcissists is a way forward from being victims to becoming survivors. With that thought in mind, let's bust some more myths and misconceptions surrounding NPD and narcissism (Greenberg, 2021).

## Myth#1: Narcissists Are Always Radiating Confidence & Charm

It is essential to understand the grandiosity, charm, confidence, and thick layer of self-assuredness are nothing but a façade—more like a defense mechanism to adapt to and shroud away the insecurities and vulnerabilities gnawing at the surface. The charm and confidence are nothing but a well-constructed and painstakingly maintained defensive façade to garner approval and applause and impress people to bolster one's diminishing self-esteem. People with NPD struggle against the fear of embarrassment and doubt and fight their overwhelming feelings of self-hate and self-contempt with a façade of confidence and poise.

## Myth#2: All Narcissists Intentionally Prey on the Emotions of Their Loved Ones

What's the biggest, most challenging struggle of living with and loving someone with NPD? Loving a narcissist is not easy, especially when you believe that they intentionally hurt, exploit and manipulate others around them. How can one forgive, love, and appreciate someone they think is deliberately and purposefully hurting them? One simply cannot; no matter how ardent and sincere the efforts.

Do narcissists genuinely want to hurt their family members and friends? They might appear to want to hurt their loved ones intentionally, but in most cases, they actually don't. Truth be told, narcissists are entirely blind to their actions and the harmful impact and destructive effects of their behavior traits. They are solely focused on addressing their emotional, physical, and material needs. They are entirely oblivious to the suffering of whoever gets hurt in the pursuit of their ambitions and agendas. This oblivion is not intentional, but rather, it stems from their lack of empathy. The term "collateral damage" is thrown around a lot while explaining the disastrous emotional damages resulting from coping with a toxic relationship with a narcissist. You are simply collateral damage in the path leading up to their ambitions and dreams.

## Myth#3: Narcissists Have a Masterful Talent for Manipulation

Here's another myth that encourages people to demonize narcissists. All narcissists are not ace manipulators, and all people with NPD do not use manipulative tactics as an emotional weapon to prey upon the vulnerabilities of others.

Some narcissists have the patience and cognitive capacity to make solid long-term plans and act them out with great secrecy and impeccable timing. But such people are scarce because most narcissists are impulsive, impatient, and stubbornly demanding. They don't prey on people with manipulative tactics, but rather, their behaviors are encouraged by people who are accommodating, indulging, and accepting of their negativity. People who erect solid and firm boundaries find it easier to escape the emotional disturbances and manipulative attempts of a narcissist.

Interestingly, many narcissists rely on "future faking" as an effective courtship strategy to woo their partners into a long-term relationship. This tactic revolves around painting an idyllic and dreamy fantasy of a romantic future they plan to have with a partner. Still, given their deep-rooted insecurities, such a future is never likely to materialize. Many narcissists are poor conversationalists, so they rely on future faking as a courtship strategy to seduce and manipulate new partners, tempting them with ideals of a romance in which they are incapable of investing. In some cases, narcissists do not use future faking to hurt or fool a lover, but rather, they end up jumping too quickly and too deep that they end up disappointing their partners. Narcissists also use future plans and fantasies as an alternative for meaningful conversations as they are often bad listeners and monopolize all discussions.

## Myth#4: All Narcissists Are Peace-Sucking Vampires Who Deliberately Prey on Their Victims

No, that is simply not true and incredibly demeaning for a person struggling against demons of their own. In today's world, where awareness of mental health conditions is available at the tip of our fingers, harboring such beliefs and misconceptions is cruel and insensitive. It is normal for a narcissist who has suffered emotional distress to look for a person to blame, and given their actions and aloofness, it's only natural for us to demonize them. But it's not a healthy response.

Narcissists deal with heightened insecurities and vulnerabilities that cause their sense of self-esteem and self-worth to fluctuate, encouraging them to seek validation, approval, and attention. Their symptoms make them insensitive and incapable of empathy, and they simply tune out the feelings, emotions, and needs of the people close to them.

Narcissists are not principally evil beings. They are unhealthy and mentally challenged people struggling to process their own emotions, thoughts, and behaviors. The negativity they radiate is the negativity they live with every single day. Dispelling myths is satisfying and a vital prerequisite on our journey to arm ourselves with facts and research to deal with narcissists positively, healthily, and constructively.

# 2

# RECOGNIZING A NARCISSIST

You can spot a narcissist easily upon entering a room, as you will always find them shining—basking in the light of attention showered upon them by an enraptured audience of eager listeners, captivated by their charm. That's what people say, but people who have lived or dealt with narcissists understand the intricate façade of charm they wear, hiding their insecurities and vulnerabilities with carefully concocted layers of realities. Contrary to what is said and written about identifying a narcissist, the process isn't easy, and there are no straight-forward formulas. That's right because every individual is different and unique. We cannot approach the study of the human mind without realizing that every human being is different and unique.

So, before we dive deeper into this chapter, I want to emphasize this point: every narcissist must be approached individually without generalizing. Yes, there are a few symptoms that are prevalent across many individuals diagnosed with NPD. Then we have the 9-step diagnostic criteria enshrined in the DSM-5 (which we will discuss shortly), but every individual with NPD is strikingly different from the other. We cannot generalize selfish behaviors, and while many people reading this book will relate to the experiences it narrates, we must understand that narcissism has many faces. Not all narcissists manifest their condition with textbook signs and symptoms. One must dig deep and look beyond the surface to recognize the deep-rooted vulnerabilities and insecurities.

This chapter will look at a broad array of symptoms and signs to show you the many faces and facets of narcissistic behavior. Why revisit the symptoms when we already covered them in the previous chapter? This time, we will explore each sign individually to understand its behavioral manifestations across different spectrums of the narcissist personality disorder.

## GENERAL NARCISSISTIC BEHAVIOR SYMPTOMS

Various common signs can help people identify traits of narcissism in their partners, parents, family members, and friends. The individual doesn't need to manifest all the signs and symptoms. The Diagnostic and Statistical Manual (DSM-5) dictates that an individual only needs to display at least five of the nine symptoms to be diagnosed with a narcissistic personality disorder. As we read through familiar-sounding signs and symptoms, it gets increasingly hard to avoid generalization. Still, we must focus and dig deeper to understand the characteristics of the narcissists in our midst.

Here are some widely observed characteristics associated with narcissistic personality disorder (Fjelstad, 2020):

## An Inflated Sense of Entitlement & Superiority

Narcissists only feel safe and confident when they are shining at the top. Their life revolves around a social hierarchy, and they always position themselves at the top, looking down at everyone with a profoundly exaggerated sense of entitlement. They strongly and firmly believe they deserve everything they desire—a belief that stems from their vivid sense of superiority. They consider themselves superhuman beings, the ultimate superheroes, and saviors with a magical touch that can turn everything into gold. In reality, it's the opposite because their constant desire to stay on top and be the most competent person pushes other people away, turning all their relationships and friendships to dust.

Narcissists cannot stand competition. They see everything along bipolar lines; it's either black or white, good or bad, right or wrong, superior or inferior. There's no middle ground. They strive to be recognized as the best, the most distinguished, and the most right, or else, they will be profoundly dissatisfied and disappointed. They want to do everything their way, because according to them, their strategies, thoughts, and plans are the best. They have an overwhelming urge to control everything and everyone. Their exaggerated sense of entitlement gives birth to an aggressive, controlling streak, and everyone around them has little choice but to obey unless they want to risk ruining their relationship by criticizing or stopping the narcissist.

Did you know that narcissists can even feed on their superiority and entitlement if they are the most wicked, most wrong, most angered, and most upset? It's perfectly normal for a narcissist to feel superior after trampling over the feelings and emotions of others. They demand others to nurse them and soothe them in times of distress but do not feel any such obligations when they are the culprits behind others' pain—which is often the case. They feel entitled to demand forgiveness, concern, and compassion. Do you know what's most hurtful and shock-ing? They feel entitled to the right to hurt others and inflict pain on their loved ones, only to demand them to make apologies and amends. This entitlement is often associated with covert or vulnerable narcissism, and narcissists take great pride in demanding apologies and amends in ways that satisfy and feed their ego.

For many of us, this sign is too relatable to ignore, and it can bring back painful memories if you've made the enor-mously challenging decision of leaving your narc. In my case, my husband's sense of entitlement and superiority remained a significant cause of friction in our relation-ship. His behavior was always powered with a strong desire to be correct and always have the last word—so much that it became an obsession. He would usurp every conversation and discussion as an opportunity to flaunt his intellect, for he loved it when people showered him with praise over his intelligence. He was a bright man, I don't deny, but his inability to handle disagreement frightened me at times. He would hold long and animated conversations, but heaven forbid if he was ever proven wrong. He wouldn't let it go for days pondering over books and the internet to do his research. And finally, after days of research, he would build his arguments and reach out to the person who disagreed with him to share his sources and validate his stance. He would go to exceptionally exhausting lengths to prove that he was right. Now, when I look back, I think the effort wasn't just to prove himself right, but rather, the goal of establishing that no one could be right other than him.

## An Insatiable Desire for Attention and Approval

Here's a core characteristic that often gives narcissists away, despite their carefully concocted layers of charm and façade: a persistent need for validation, attention, and praise. If you've lived with a narcissist, here's a common trait: they're constantly trailing you around, making demands, asking you to run errands, find missing items or absolutely anything to become the constant subject of your attention.

Narcissists have an unbelievable hunger for validation, and this hunger is truly never-ending. Interestingly, validation only counts for them when it comes from others.

Unlike most people, narcissists cannot bolster their ego and self-esteem but rely on others to do it for them. Ironically enough, even showering them with praise and attention isn't enough to win over their gratitude, love, or attention. Most people, especially children, find the struggle of praising and validating narcissists heartbreaking because no matter how grand their gestures are, their efforts are just never enough. A narcissist's hunger for praise, attention, and validation is like a bottomless well, and no matter how much positivity, recognition, support, and kind words you pour in, the well will never fill up. It's as if the gestures of support and compassion are forgotten within seconds, and they start demanding more.

No matter how sincerely and frequently you tell them that you admire them, love them, respect them or believe in them, words are simply lost because deep down, in their hearts, they genuinely believe that no one can ever love, respect, or admire them. You see, this deep-rooted trait that only the closest can identify unveils all the insecurities, paranoia, fear, and vulnerabilities hiding beneath the façade of grandiose, superiority, and entitlement. They want to secure praise, approval, and validation more than anything because approval works like a band-aid to support their fragmented ego and fragile self-esteem. And the vicious cycle never stops because the more you give, the more they demand.

## The Unwavering Pursuit of Perfectionism

This is an easy one, and I'm sure everyone can relate to the narcissist's passion for perfectionism. They thrive on the belief that they are the absolute best, and everything they create is a magnificent specimen of perfectionism. A narcissist's exaggerated need for perfectionism can make others extraordinarily uncomfortable and inconvenienced. They pursue perfectionism with the utmost dedication and devotion that can scare others away.

Narcissists firmly believe that everything they plan or do should map out exactly how they have envisioned it. They cannot tolerate any alterations or changes to their plans, no matter how big or small these changes may be. They believe in precision and accuracy, be it work, relationships, or life. Narcissists believe in perfection and demand the same from others. They think they are perfect, and they require everyone around them to be perfect too. Events should be perfect, food should be perfect, projects should be perfect—each and everything thing they do must shine with perfection.

Perfectionism is a flaw within itself, and it is indeed an impossible demand to make of oneself, let alone anyone else. Narcissists pursue perfection, and more often than not, this pursuit leaves them feeling empty, deeply dissatisfied, and devastatingly miserable. They are always complaining about how things didn't go their way or how things would be better if they were in charge of everything with their spectacular brand of perfectionism.

I can tell from experience that dealing with a narcissist's demands for perfectionism is endlessly exhausting and will devour every ounce of your mental energy. My husband considered himself a man of many skills, and he claimed excellence in all his capabilities and talents. His bartending skills were indeed the finest jewel in his crown of talents, and he didn't let a single opportunity to showcase his bartending abilities go to waste. I remember the creative drinks he would create to 'wow' all our friends with his exceptional talents. As fun and enjoyable as this experience sounds, it wasn't—because the pressure and stress to consume the drinks precisely the way he wanted us to was too much of a challenge for everyone.

You see, he wouldn't just seek praise and approval, but rather, he forced us to drink his creations precisely the way he had planned to ensure a night of successful execution for the plans he laid with such perfection!

He loved being showered with praise, but heaven forbid if any one of us would start a conversation or take our time finishing up the chilled drink. He would rush and immediately nudge to finish up before the ice melts and the drink gets diluted, ruining the flavor he created for us to enjoy. After pondering over his behavior for years, I finally understood that the stress he created for us on those nights of strict entertainment stemmed from his fear of negativity. He was afraid his guests would make negative comments about his drinks if they didn't enjoy them properly. His deep-rooted concern for the opinion of others encouraged him to pursue perfectionism or agonize and moan over his perceived failures.

## An Uncontrollable Need to Dominate Everyone

Narcissists are easily recognizable by their desire to control everyone and everything. They have an aggressive dominating streak, and they believe their perfection and sense of superiority makes them the right person to take the lead and guide others along the way. It's important to note that narcissists are perpetually discontent with imperfections and events that don't go their way, so they decide to take things into their hands and stubbornly refuse to give control to others around them.

They want to control every small and significant aspect of their lives and ensure every outcome is favorable and precisely as they envisioned. They fiercely and stubbornly demand control, and people who want to live with them and wholeheartedly support them always find themselves being dominated and controlled excessively. A narcissist's sense of entitlement and superiority makes it perfectly logical for them to be the one in control of everything—especially the life of their family and loved ones.

They make decisions and process emotions based on their mental narrative, for they have concocted stories and characters and demand everyone to act precisely as their mental narrative dictates. They want to dictate what a person says, does, or thinks, so much so that it gets hard to voice their thoughts—let alone demand one's right to make one's own choices and decisions. They require total control to ensure that the outcomes are just as they planned in their heads. The people around them, be it family members, friends, or colleagues, are simply characters in their story, and these characters must do precisely what they are told. Any deviations from the storyline can anger the narcissist, triggering a chain of incredibly upsetting and chaotic events. If you've lived with a narcissist, you understand their controlling streak only too well, and you also know that the slightest resistance to bend their will is always met with bitter contempt and blatant disregard for your feelings.

This particular sign is too real and raw for me, and for the longest time, my life with my husband was a constant struggle and an unsatisfied yearning for freedom. Surprisingly, now that I think about it, I didn't ask for a lot of space, just the small things here and there that make us feel in control of our lives. I didn't have the freedom to buy simple things for our home as innocuous choices undoubtedly turned into long, drawn-out conversations. Even purchasing something as menial as a tissue box holder for our master bathroom resulted in a much longer discussion than necessary.

One day, he brought home a tissue box holder for our master bathroom, and I was not too fond of the design. It took me hours to ransack my brain for an appropriate, polite, and respectful way to express my opinion constructively. I wanted to be truthful and share my opinion. Still, the fear of upsetting him and unleashing his narcissistic rage was always too much to risk, given that I was also raising three young boys and wanted to maintain a healthy home environment. But that day, after much effort and planning, I finally expressed my opinion. Let me mention here that he wasn't in the habit of asking for my views unless he wanted me to praise him for his commendable choices. That day, he wanted me to praise him, but instead, I calmly said, "Well, it's not what I would've chosen."

I tried to frame my words as delicately and sensitively as possible without deviating from my truth or sounding disapproving. But his response was grossly disrespectful of my right to voice my opinion. My truthful response had triggered an aggressive fit of rage, and he yelled, "Well, next time, you buy it then!" I tried to calm him down and explain how much care and thought I put into sharing my opinion, but he simply didn't register my thoughts and continued to regard it as an insult or criticism of his choices, and therefore, his person.

When I finally decided to part ways and resurrected my life and personality, one of the greatest joys that I discovered was the freedom to buy everything I liked without having to run into exhausting arguments over petty things. One may not believe it, but the ability to buy what one wants is essential to bolster one's self-image and confidence. Realizing that my opinions and choices mattered boosted my confidence tremendously. Gaining freedom from his ridiculous and unnecessary arguments has been one of the greatest victories of my life—absolutely priceless!

## Blame Games & Deflection to Escape Responsibility

A narcissist's lack of responsibility is excruciatingly hard to ignore in any relationship, be it as a colleague, a friend, a sibling, a parent, and especially, as a spouse. It's hard to patch things up with them or mend ties in any way because their persistent pursuit of control and always wanting to emerge as the shining hero of their story deters them from taking responsibility for their actions. They can take responsibility, but only as a tactic to get what they want or trigger a response in the other person to achieve their desired results. In the event of things not going the way they planned, the narcissist will conveniently shift the blame and leave you feeling responsible for everything in an attempt to sustain their image of perfection and escape criticism.

It always has to be someone else's mistake. Narcissists will never let accusing fingers point towards them. If the blame is generalized, they will believe that everyone is plotting a malignant agenda against them rather than realizing their own mistakes. In most cases, narcissists find it easier to blame people who are closest to them and love them the most. People who are most loyal and accommodating and shower them with love and respect are unfortunately most likely to carry the burdens of their mistakes and errors. Narcissists will do anything and everything to sustain their façade of superiority and perfection, even if it's done at your expense. They don't have much trouble trampling over the trust and commitment they receive from others, and the people who are unlikely to leave or criticize them are the safest people to blame.

Lack of responsibility and vicious blame games play into everyday situations in the most bizarre ways, leaving you drained of all energies and strength. I remember I used to be in charge of all the grocery shopping around the house, and we had a monthly budget that I had planned in a manner to feed my family of five comfortably. One month, my husband accused me of splurging too much and going over budget. I respectfully reminded him that he had overspent on alcohol that month, and as soon as he realized that he was the one to blame for our overspending, he completely shifted the blame and changed the argument. Suddenly, he started accusing me of mistreating him so much that he had to "self-medicate his depression" by drowning his sorrows in liquor.

His ability to turn the tables and shift the blame was so manipulative and masterful that I never had a chance to compose myself and respond. With time, I realized that disagreeing with him will only invite more hostility, for he was incapable of having a civilized conversation, and I rarely got a chance to disagree with him without unleashing his belligerent narcissistic rage. He opposed criticism and would belittle me if I dared to voice opinions that contradicted his.

He would leave me feeling stupid regarding my thoughts and opinions, and I learned to stop sharing views that contradicted his. I simply didn't have the energy to argue over anything big or small, and like all victims, I learned to stay silent and shoulder the blame to avoid ruffling the feathers of my narc. As the years went by, my silence and passiveness resulted in a profoundly damaging loss of sense, and when I finally left him, I had to rebuild my life piece by piece, relearn everything, and find myself all over again. I managed to rejuvenate and invigorate myself, but the aftershocks of the emotional trauma still make me hesitant while voicing my opinions and sharing my truth.

## No Concept of Emotional Boundaries

Crossing someone's boundaries isn't deviance until it becomes a norm or a habit. Narcissists commonly exhibit "status-quo" behavior, and they breeze through life without respecting or even recognizing the boundaries of others. This is primarily why people accuse them of exhibiting child-like behavior. They often act like little children who believe they are entitled to everything and can do whatever they please without any consequences. They believe that everyone holds the same feelings and emotions as them, and everyone will want the same things they desire.

Showing narcissists the reality is nearly impossible, for they are not accustomed to hearing the word 'no.' They feel insulted and rejected when people deny them what they want. A narcissist will go to great lengths of plotting, scheming, and planning if they desire something from you, and you decide to withhold it or show resistance to their demands. Their scheming will begin with careful persistence, moving towards cajoles and concealed threats, aggressive demands, heartbreaking rejections, and finally, pouting and whining until they get what they want.

## An Acute Inability to Empathize with Others

Here's a core narcissistic trait that often encourages us to demonize our narcs and paint them as the villains they often appear to be. We all know that's not a healthy and positive choice, and we must steer away from toxic generalizations by understanding a narcissist's lack of empathy.

Narcissists have very little or no empathy to give others. Lack of empathy is a trademark sign of narcissism, recognized by unbelievable selfishness, self-absorption, and self-centeredness. They never stop to think and regard situations from the perspectives of others around them, but they stubbornly demand everyone to experience, feel, and think exactly the way they do. Narcissists hardly spare a thought to the feelings and desires of others, and they display their lack of empathy without any semblance of remorse, guilt, or blame.

Experts from the University of Warsaw explain that many people with NPD do not have concrete concepts of feelings and emotions (Zajenkowski et al., 2018). They simply don't understand the nature and dynamics of human feelings and how they occur. Usually, they blame others for their feelings. They don't think their feelings stem from their mind but rather regard their emotions as an external effort caused by someone else other than themselves.

They don't understand that our emotions and feelings are a product of chemical and biological interactions within our brain.

Simply put, amongst all the other things, narcissists also blame others for making them feel and think the way they do. If they're disappointed, angry, or depressed, they will quickly find someone to blame for not following their plan, criticizing them, or undermining their intellect. It's excruciatingly hard to build any kind of emotional connection or embark on a rewarding relationship with a narcissist because of their blatant lack of empathy and compassion. They are utterly blind to the feelings of others.

My husband's lack of empathy was the most prominent trait that pushed me away from him. I found it extremely hard to understand his lack of empathy towards those who truly deserved our compassion. Even I, his partner for life and the mother of his children, was not deserving of his empathy, care, and compassion.

I remember attending one therapy session with him in an attempt to mend our relationship, and I started crying inconsolably while he sat there, completely unaffected and unfazed. The therapist quickly noticed that the behaviors and memories that made me so upset had little or no impact on him. When she asked him why he didn't seem affected, he casually remarked, "She does this all the time." Up until that point, I had dodged many canons and ignored many red flags, but at that moment, the realization truly dawned upon me that there was not an ounce of care in his heart—not a trace of remorse for my suffering!

But what truly disgusted and shocked me was his disregard and lack of empathy towards the victims of the 9/11 attacks. I recall us watching the devastating scenes of the Twin Towers crumbling down, and I remember feeling broken and speechless over the unprecedented loss of life that we were watching on our TV screen. I couldn't stop the tears from rolling down, and as soon as he saw me crying, he coldly remarked, "You probably don't know any of them anyway."

I learned to stop sharing my emotions and feelings the hard way; after being burned and rejected over and over, I realized and quietly accepted that he will never understand how to support my feelings and engage with my emotions. He was so self-absorbed in his own needs and desires that he would routinely put his needs over those of our beautiful children. I always had my hands full taking care of my three boys, but he didn't see all the effort I was putting in and would always try to monopolize my attention. It constantly felt as if he always wanted me to be there for him, to attend to his needs only, while ignoring our children.

## Feeling Threatened by Everything & Everyone

Narcissists have a highly sensitive radar for perceiving threats, rejection, and anger, and they are the masters of misreading expressions and perceiving negativity from others. They are incredibly biased and very crafty at turning things around by sensing harm, rejection, and negativity from others. Interestingly, narcissists are unable to accurately understand the emotions of others unless you present them with a dramatic outburst of your emotions.

At times, even the things you do to make amends or burn the hatches, dropping apologies, and confessing your love can make them edgy, angry, and frustrated. They refuse to believe declarations of love and misread every statement you make as an attack or a threat to their person. It's natural for narcissists to get defensive and respond with negativity, especially in jokes and sarcasm. They often misinterpret jokes as personal attacks.

**Inability to Understand Logic & Reasoning**

Have you ever tried reasoning and using logic to justify your actions and feelings to a narcissist? I have, and each effort has always been met with no success and a barrage of insults, criticism, and negativity. It's impossible to make them understand the consequences of their actions on your mental well-being and the pain they have caused you. A rational person would think that communicating is the key to every relationship, and healthy people reconsider their actions when they've realized the pain and hurt they've caused. That's not the case with a narcissist, and the sooner you grasp this reality, the better you can deal with their manipulative attacks.

Narcissists cannot process or understand emotional reasoning and logical explanations, as they are only attuned to their own feelings and reasonings. Even if they say they understand your perspective, don't fall for the scam, for it's just a tactic to smooth out the tension temporarily.

It's essential to understand that their feelings and desires drive the decision-making process of a narcissist. If they want to buy something, they will buy it because of their feelings associated with that purchase, rather than the benefits it will bring for their family and household. If they are bored, they will walk out of a relationship, if they feel uninspired, they will walk out of a job and find something new, and if they are angry, they will lash out in whatever ways help them feel powerful and calm. They cannot solve and address their feelings and seek outside help, constantly expecting others to comply with their commands and orders.

## A Tendency to Split Everything between Good & Bad

Splitting is by far one of the most disturbing and manipulative traits of a narcissist, and it divides their mind and personality into two spheres: good and bad. Therefore, they split everything in their life and their relationships into two sides, good and bad. Naturally, all the negativity they encounter in life is blamed on others, especially the closest people, and they graciously take credit for all the positivity and goodness.

They are in constant denial of their negativity and hurtful actions and readily accuse others of denying their goodness. It's extremely challenging for narcissists to find a middle ground or blend the constructs of good and bad to have a meaningful experience. Each experience they have is either fabulous and good or terrible and bad.

One example of splitting is how my husband dealt with politics. He had extreme views, and those who agreed with him were labeled "good," and those who didn't were labeled "bad." There was no compromise or attempt to see the other side when it opposed his hardline views on issues. Everything was black and white. Simply no grey area in the way he saw politics and life, in general.

### Fear of Being Ridiculed & Rejected by Others

Fear is a recurring emotion that dominates the life, thoughts, and feelings of a narcissist. One must dig really deep to understand the fear that motivates, consumes, and drives a narcissist, for it is buried and repressed deep within the carefully concocted layers of their personality. Narcissists are driven by a fear of being rejected, ridiculed, or proven wrong. Many fears engulf their mind, but of all the fears they struggle against, the fear of rejection and ridicule motivates and consumes them the most.

We've already established that all narcissists are different, and they experience many fears. Some are afraid of contracting germs. Others are afraid of losing their youthfulness and beauty, being physically or emotionally abused, of loneliness, and being seen as the villain rather than the victim. All these fears make it impossible for the narcissist to trust anyone around them.

Most people fail to realize that the closer you get, the less and less narcissists will trust you. At the core, narcissists are drowning in fear of vulnerability, intimacy and allowing their weaknesses and imperfections to appear on the surface. They wear a carefully crafted façade of perfection, and they don't want anyone to take a peek beneath the mask in fear of rejection, criticism, and judgment. The biggest irony is that no amount of praise, adoration, and reassurance can remedy their confidence and help them develop trust in the people who love them and want to help them. Deep down, they are deeply ashamed of themselves, and they truly hate their weaknesses and imperfections. The fear of rejection encourages them to test people with negativity, hurtfulness, and behaviors that bring their loved ones to a breaking point.

**Uncontrollable Bouts of Anxiety**

Anxiety is a perpetual and never-ending companion for narcissists, occupying their minds with the fear that something terrible is about to dismantle their peace. Anxiety manifests itself differently in every narcissist. Some manifest anxiety by incessantly talking about the bad things that will shatter their lives, while others try to repress and conceal their anxiety.

In most cases, narcissists unburden their anxiety onto their closest family members and loved ones. They accuse their loved ones of being mentally unwell, not fulfilling their emotional needs, not supporting them adequately, and wronging them. These accusations help the narcissist transfer and project their anxiety onto the people around them.

Understand this carefully: narcissists feel better, uplifted, and powerful when they project their anxiety onto others and leave those in their wake to feel negative, insulted, and belittled. It makes them feel stronger, powerful, and superior when they watch the people closest to them drowning in depression, anxiety and stress.

**Deep-rooted Guilt & Shame**

Narcissists are incapable of feeling guilty because, in their minds, they are the one true embodiment of everything pure, righteous, and heroic in this world. They don't believe they can ever cause harm to anyone, but deep down, they are drowning in shame. Narcissists are constantly drowning in the shame of their fears, insecurities, rejections, and vulnerabilities that they work so hard to hide from others, mainly themselves. Their deeply repressed shame drives their lives and thoughts, and it takes a Herculean amount of effort for them to continue feeding their false sense of self-esteem. Ultimately, their crafted image of self makes it impossible for them to offer transparency in any relationship.

**Inability to Get Intimate & Vulnerable with Loved Ones**

Narcissists are unempathetic, and their failure to comprehend feelings, coupled with their perpetual need to protect themselves, renders them completely unable to be vulnerable and form intimate, emotional connections with people. They are incapable of viewing the world from the perspectives of others, and their emotional neediness makes it impossible for their loved ones to give them the sense of security and admiration they desire.

It's natural for narcissists to break out of unsatisfying relationships or start a new one without ending an existing relationship. They desperately want to play the victim and share their pain and suffering with others to garner sympathy. Their brand of codependency demands empathy, admiration, and an abundance of compassion for their perceived disadvantages, but narcissists will not spare a second to understand and respond to your needs.

**Poor Communication & Team Coordination Skills**

Narcissists are unable to work as team players who support, coordinate and communicate with others effectively. You see, cooperation requires an understanding and a respectful attitude towards the feelings and needs of others. When a person is incapable of identifying and respecting the feeling of others, they are incapable of working towards shared goals and objectives. Their competitive, obsessive and demanding streaks make it difficult for others to work with them, for they are only striving for their benefits.

My husband struggled to enjoy satisfaction in his work, and his possessive and dominating streak would also interfere with his work relationships. On one nonsensical occasion, he was planning the seating arrangement for a company meeting, and he was adamant that one of his female colleagues should sit exactly where he had planned for her to sit. She wasn't comfortable sitting there, stood her ground that she decided to sit where she pleased, but he became furious and insisted that she move to sit where he had told her to sit.

## DSM-5 CRITERIA: DIAGNOSING NARCISSISTIC PERSONALITY DISORDER (NPD)

The Diagnostic and Statistical Manual of Mental Disorders (DSM-5) lays down comprehensive criteria to diagnose someone with NPD. The DSM outlines nine personality traits, and a person must meet at least five of these traits to be diagnosed with NPD (Cunha, 2020).

**These nine traits are:**

1. An exaggerated sense of self-significance.
2. A continual obsession with fantasies of grandeur, beauty, ideal romance, intellectual brilliance, power, or unrivaled success.
3. An obsession that they are special and unique beings and can only connect and be understood by people who share such high status and superiority.
4. A constant, never-ending need for admiration.
5. An inflated sense of entitlement.
6. An exploitative and manipulative personality— ability to take advantage of their loved ones.

7. Inability to empathize or understand feelings.
8. Jealousy or the belief that others are jealous of them.
9. Haughtiness and arrogance.

## OVERT VS. COVERT NARCISSISM

Human behaviors are described as overt or covert in psychology, and as we established earlier, NPD manifests itself in overt and covert forms (Clarke, 2020). This section will take a closer look at the overt and covert forms of NPD behaviors.

Overt behaviors are easy to identify and observe, much like the traditional behaviors of a typical narcissist discussed above. Still, covert behaviors are less evident and hard to follow because of their subtlety and tact.

A covert narcissist is an individual who acts differently from an overt narcissist and secretly yearns for significance and admiration, with an acute lack of empathy. When one imagines and revisits the behavior traits, it's hard to imagine a subtle and restrained narcissist. However, covert narcissists will surprise you with their self-effacing behaviors and withdrawn approach while silently working towards the same goal of self-glorification at the expense of others.

**Overt Narcissism**

To differentiate, we can regard overt narcissists as people with more pronounced and observable traits, while covert narcissists are more subtle and discreet. Overt narcissists are easy to identify because of their boisterous, loud, unempathetic, arrogant attitudes and insatiable hunger for admiration. It's easy to spot them in a room, basking in the light of attention and wrapping up a "big" audience around their animated tales of bravado and brilliance. An easy way to spot overt narcissists is by their extroverted personalities and their boisterous and enthusiastic interactions with people around them.

**Covert Narcissism**

Subtly and introversion are the only traits that differentiate covert narcissists from their overt counterparts. However, the term covert does not indicate that narcissists are sneaky, and their behaviors are not as troubling and damaging as those of overt narcissists. The underlying traits and drives of both overt and covert narcissists are similar.

**Overt vs. Covert: Keeping up with Traits & Behaviors**

Essentially, both overt and covert narcissists live their lives with a heightened sense of self-significance and grand fantasies of success, power, beauty, and wealth. To be diagnosed with NPD, both overt and covert narcissists must meet the DSM-5 criteria, regardless of their introverted or extroverted personalities.

It is easier for victims to be manipulated and exploited by covert narcissists without realizing the manipulative behaviors until they are exposed to emotional suffering and pain. It's fair to conclude that overt narcissists are easier to spot than their introverted, covert counterparts. People often embark on long-term relationships, marriage, and work arrangements with covert narcissists without realizing their traits, until their lack of reciprocity and sensitivity becomes too difficult to ignore. Victims are left questioning their intelligence and wondering how they could possibly fall for a narcissist. The analogy of the frog in a pot of water is often used to explain how this all came to be. If you try to put a frog into a pot of hot water, it will immediately jump out. However, if you put a frog into a pot of room temperature water, it will sit there and remain there as the heat is turned up. Before the frog realizes how hot the water is, the damage has been done. Much is the same with being in a relationship with a covert narcissist.

## Identifying a Covert Narcissist

Here are some traits that will help you identify and deal with a covert narcissist before getting caught up in exploitative drama and manipulation (Clarke, 2020).

## Procrastination and Disregard

Covert narcissists are consumed with perceived notions of their self-importance and grandeur, and they will do whatever it takes to make sure they are always the shining beacon of attention. They refuse to share attention with anyone, especially those that they claim to love dearly. While an overt narcissist will manipulate, exploit, and disregard you blatantly, the covert narc has a much more masterful strategy: they simply refuse to acknowledge your existence and the existence of your feelings and emotions. These people are drawn towards empathetic, caring, and compassionate people to feed on these emotions and fulfill their needs for admiration and validation.

## Emotionally Neglectful

Covert narcissists are emotionally neglectful, and they feel little remorse about making little of the hurt, pain, and suffering of others. This trait is shared across all narcissists, but it manifests itself with an acute inability to be emotionally healthy in covert narcissists. These narcissists may appear more agreeable, kind, and compassionate than overt narcs, but they are just as unsympathetic and emotionally inaccessible.

## Giving with a Goal

Everything that covert narcissists do is a means to an end that results in them being glorified and showered with praise and admiration. They do and give with a goal, and the goal usually revolves around their inflated ego and sense of superiority. Everything they do is aligned with their agendas to enjoy the results they have planned so meticulously. When you see them showering you with attention, praise or gifts, understand that they want something from you and will deploy every tactic in their handbook to get what they want.

## MALIGNANT NARCISSISM – THE MOST DESTRUCTIVE FORM OF NARCISSISM

Malignant narcissism is the most damaging and destructive form of narcissism, and recognizing these narcissists is instrumental because they typically enjoy great significance and esteem in their social circles. They are held in overly high regard and respect by everyone who knows them because they have a masterful ability to paint a magical picture of virtues, charm, and compassion that people can't help but fall in love with and admire. But when you dig deeper and scratch the surface relentlessly, you find a personality drowning in self-absorption with a maliciously dark side, willing to expose you to unimaginable trauma to achieve their goals.

Malignant narcissists are the most dangerous and damaging narcissists, and they embody all the traits and symptoms of a textbook narcissist. But aside from their monstrously enormous ego, they also exhibit signs of antisocial behavior, a distorted and vague sense of self, an acute lack of empathy, and a damaging sadistic side. Malignant narcissism is often associated with paranoia and fear. Many experts point out there are very few differences between psychopaths and malignant narcissists, given that both exhibit a lack of empathy and antisocial traits (Scott, 2020).

## Recognizing Malignant Narcissism

These narcissists are dangerously manipulative, and they don't care who they trample, drown and dismantle in the pursuit of their goals and agendas (Scott, 2020).

**Some other traits include:**

- A black and white worldview where people are either their friends or their sworn enemies.
- An obsession with winning, no matter the cost. They have little regard for the pain, suffering, and anger their actions cause to others.
- A general disregard and nonchalance about the pain and suffering they bring to others—in fact, they seem to extract their power from hurting and disturbing others.
- They strive hard and aggressively to prevent any inconvenience, hardship, or loss from befalling them.
- They always find a way to manipulate others and take advantage of people to get what they want.
- They show little remorse for their mistakes and the pain they've caused, and they only apologize in situations that serve their plans.
- They tend to monopolize conversations, denying others the chance to speak and express themselves.
- A tendency to mistreat the people they regard as inferior.

- They resort to blaming others for their own destructive and damaging actions.

**Diagnosing & Spotting a Malignant Narcissist**

Identifying and diagnosing a malignant narcissist isn't easy because this form is often overlapping with several other severe psychiatric conditions. However, the official diagnostic criteria enshrined in the DSM-5 serve as the clinical methodology, even though malignant narcissism isn't explicitly mentioned in the manual.

Typically, the term malignant narcissism is used to describe a person with the following conditions:

- Narcissistic personality disorder (NPD)
- Antisocial personality disorder (APD)
- Paranoia and fear
- Sadism
- Aggression

People with malignant narcissism are just that, malignant, and they exploit and manipulate others for amusement. The experience of depriving others of their power, self-esteem, and safety is amusing for them, and it empowers them, fueling their deep-rooted insecurities and vulnerabilities with a dynamic sense of control that makes them feel good and strong.

# 3

# THE RELATIONSHIP BETWEEN NARCISSISM AND CODEPENDENCY

I t's hard to talk about living and dealing with narcissism without approaching the complex and interlaced subject of codependency. When seen in a healthy and normal environment, relying on our loved ones for emotional, mental, and spiritual support isn't such a bad thing, right? But in our relationships with narcissists, codependency plays out in the most damaging of ways. I firmly believe that when one is dealing with the complex and erratic personality of a narcissist, the closure of understanding psychological terminologies and insights is immensely beneficial. It opens and expands the mind, and everything that was once a parade of glaring questions gnawing at your brain becomes amazingly clear, and you start understanding why your narcissist did what they did to hurt you and bring you pain.

In this chapter, we will be talking about narcissism and codependent behaviors of the victims and the narcissists. Did you know that narcissists are drawn towards codependent victims who have a nurturing and compassionate nature? That's right, and it's common for the victims of narcissistic abuse to exhibit codependent tendencies. In other cases, narcissists can also start manifesting signs of codependency. If you're struggling to catch up, don't worry, we will make this easier, starting by breaking down codependency and what it entails.

## WHAT IS CODEPENDENCY?

Codependency refers to a deep-rooted need to seek physical, emotional, mental, or spiritual dependence on anyone—a family member, a partner, or a friend (Gould, 2020). Keep in mind that codependency is not a psychological condition or a clinical problem. Instead, it is a mental state of vulnerability that often takes root from adverse childhood experiences. While codependence isn't a significant psychological concern, it can make a person increasingly vulnerable, mentally challenged, and reliant on others. Eventually, if codependent behaviors are not controlled and discouraged, they can develop into a dependent personality disorder.

Interestingly, the term was first introduced during the 1950s to offer support to the partners of individuals involved in substance abuse (Rosenberg, 2013) because these partners were caught up in the toxic traits and damaging lifestyles. While codependency involves a wide array of attributes and conditions, this much remains true: codependents end up being caught up in the trauma, turmoil, and toxic traits of selfishly dominating personalities.

So, what is codependency? It involves a series of attachment and reliance patterns, most of which a child develops during the early years of infancy. It manifests itself in a broad spectrum of forms, shapes, and sizes, and each form comes with a distinctive intensity. Fundamentally, codependency stems from a vague sense of self, lack of effective boundaries, lack of opinions, and most importantly, an inability to say no. Interestingly, codependency can emerge in any relationship dynamic, be it a relationship between a parent and a child, two partners or spouses, a boss and subordinate or even two colleagues.

**Signs & Traits**

Like we've discussed, codependency involves a series of imbalanced and boundaryless attachment patterns where the responsibility of satisfying a person's need falls entirely on you, without any regard for your feelings and needs. Codependents fuel the enormous ego of their narcissists and nurture and care for their needs without considering their own desires and needs. It can be seen as a circular pattern of attachment where a person needs another person, and that other person just wants to feel needed. The codependent, who is the giver, will feel powerless, worthless, and unimportant unless required, loved, and praised by the taker or the enabler. The giver will make sacrifice after sacrifice, ready to put their head on a stake, just to feel needed and wanted by the taker. It's a toxic pattern, and the codependent sacrifices everything while the taker thrives on the power stemming from the vulnerabilities and low self-esteem of the giver.

All healthy relationships are formed on a balance of power and an active decision to share this power to feel empowered and happy together. Codependent relationships are toxic and unhealthy as they revolve around an unequal power. Essentially, the relationship dynamics revolve around the needs and desires of the taker. At the same time, the giver must strive hard, making sacrifices to display and prove their love and fulfilling the whims and wishes of the taker.

Here are some signs of codependency (Mental Health America, n.d.):

- A constant need to ask permission from the other person before performing any menial or significant task.
- An overwhelming feeling of avoiding mistakes to prevent conflict and angering the other person.
- An overpowering urge and need to rescue or change unhealthy, addicted, troubled, and toxic people and whose challenges and issues are beyond an average person's ability to address them.
- Always apologizing to maintain peace, regardless

of whether it's your fault or theirs.

- Feeling sad and sorry for the person who has hurt you.
- Disregarding your discomfort and pain for the sake of doing anything the other person has demanded of you.
- A tendency to put the other person high up on a pedestal to worship their goodness, completely ignoring the fact that they do not deserve such esteem.
- A need to be liked by others to enjoy high self-esteem and maintain a positive image of self.
- A constant struggle to make time for your own needs.
- Constantly using your free time to do things for the other person.
- Difficulty to find yourself within a relationship and feeling as if your entire life revolves around your relationship with that person.

## Questionnaire to Identify Signs of Codependency

Wondering if you might be codependent? Codependency runs on a spectrum, rather than positive and negative for the condition. In addition to the list of symptoms above, the following questions might help you determine if you may fall on the spectrum (Mental Health America, n.d.). If you feel that you might be codependent, consulting a qualified professional is highly recommended and necessary for a formal diagnosis.

1. Do you avoid conflict by choosing to be silent?
2. Do other peoples' opinions of you affect how you express yourself?
3. Has anyone you lived with have a problem with drugs or alcohol?
4. Has anyone you lived with physically or emotionally abused you?
5. Do you value others' opinions more than your own opinions?
6. Do you find yourself having problems dealing with change in your home or work environment?
7. Does your significant other make you feel abandoned when they choose to spend time with others?
8. Do you struggle with self-doubt?
9. Do you have difficulty being honest about your opinions when speaking to others?
10. Do you feel deficient?
11. Have you ever felt bad when you are at fault?
12. Do you struggle with receiving presents or kind words of praise?
13. Are you embarrassed when those close to you mess up?
14. Are you responsible for the well-being of those closest to you?
15. Have you ever wanted someone to be your personal assistant to accomplish more during the day?
16. Do you feel intimidated when speaking with people who hold power (authority figures)?

17. Are you puzzled about what your future might hold?
18. Do you find it challenging to say no to others when they ask for your assistance?
19. Would you rather do something yourself instead of asking for assistance?
20. Are you often working on multiple projects simultaneously and unable to do any of them well?

If you found yourself answering 'yes' to many of the questions above, it might serve you well to discuss them with a qualified therapist.

**What Makes Codependency Toxic and Unhealthy?**

Codependency gives rise to an unhealthy, toxic, manipulative, and exploitative relationship dynamic, where you are constantly draining yourself of energy, happiness, joy, compassion, and care to feed the other person, who, unsurprisingly, will never be satisfied. We all have an unbelievable amount of love to share with our family, partners, spouses, children, and friends. We feel responsible for the people we love, and we care for them. We are willing and ready to take a bullet for our partner and our closest friends . . . so does that make us codependents? Absolutely not!

You see, while we are all willing to do what it takes to love and care for our loved ones, we all have boundaries and limits. And we expect our partners to reciprocate the same emotions, feelings, care, and appreciation, and a failure on their part will naturally result in retaliation on our part.

Codependency is unhealthy, toxic, and vulnerable because someone's sense of self and identity relies upon another person's adoration and love. It's vital to understand that codependency doesn't refer to our desire to love others and care for them. Still, it is just an excessive depiction of love and care, especially disregarding one's own needs and priorities. A healthy relationship is one where we are responsible for ourselves, just as we feel responsible for our partner, parent, sibling, child, or friend. Our love for ourselves must coexist freely and healthily with our love for others that we hold dear.

This unhealthy and toxic relationship dynamic is often termed "relationship addiction," and there couldn't be a more apt terminology to refer to this emotionally exploitative, abusive, manipulative, and one-sided relationship. What is the biggest problem with codependency? The giver always ends up losing their self-image and sense of identity because they end up pouring all their heart, mind, body, and soul into loving and caring for someone else more than themselves. This desire to care so much for someone else that you end up losing your sense of self is the most damaging trait of codependency.

A giver may not feel lost, drained, and empty initially, for the giver truly enjoys showering their partner with love and the idea of being needed by someone. However, it doesn't take long for the relationship dynamic to become abusive and exploitative. As the relationship progresses, the giver continues to give and give until they have lost everything that individualized and identified them except their unhealthy and toxic relationship.

It becomes increasingly challenging for the giver to disentangle themselves from a toxic relationship to make matters worse. They end up getting so emotionally and mentally caught up in the idea of another person relying on them for all their needs, even when they start realizing that their relationship isn't healthy and staying wouldn't be the right decision to make. Naturally, the taker becomes so comfortable and reliant on the giver that it's difficult for them to extricate themselves too. So, the toxic relationship eventually becomes a vicious trap for both the taker and the giver.

But, how is all this relevant to dealing with narcissists? Let's find out, shall we?

## CODEPENDENCY AND NARCISSISM

Codependency and narcissism often go hand in glove for these two personalities that may seem polar opposites but have something in common: low self-esteem and a vague sense of self (Glass, 2020). Codependents struggle to pay attention to and recognize their own needs because they are obsessed with prioritizing and fulfilling the needs of others. Interestingly, they fulfill their emotional requirements and buffer up their self-esteem by relying on other people.

They find meaningful rewards and values in caring for and helping other people, even if this help costs them their emotional, mental, and physical well-being. Their inherent and continuous desire to feel needed and wanted fuels their priorities, denying them the abilities of self-care and self-love. They live to help and serve others, and they end up feeling unwanted and worthless if they don't have a person in their lives who constantly needs them to do things for them.

This relationship isn't about love. It's about fulfilling needs and total obedience without any questions or arguments. Doesn't this sound familiar to those who have lived with or are living with narcissists? Narcissists and codependents are attracted to one another, and together, they form a perfect combination because each has a role to play that fits their inherent desires. Narcissists live to be the shining beacon of attention, to be regarded as the superhuman entity that does no wrong and ends up as the hero in every story. Narcissists are attracted to codependents because only these givers can give them the adoration they desire and admire them as if the sun shines right out of their faces. The narcissist wants nothing more than a person who puts their needs and desires above anything else, and they find this person in codependents—victims ready and willing to be manipulated, exploited, and abused in every conceivable manner, as long as they are feeling needed by another person.

A codependent does a fabulous job of feeding the narcissist's ego, boosting their self-esteem, and showering them with admiration. The codependent is more than happy to serve the role of the compassionate, selfless, nurturing, and ardent admirer, willing to dance at every whim of the narcissist.

## Understanding the Attraction between Narcissists & Codependents

Have you seen any couples where one person is overly dominant and in control of the relationship, and the other person constantly feels like they are walking on eggshells to avoid the contempt, anger, and ire of their partner? I have lived and survived such a relationship, and I am sure many of you can relate, and this struggle has brought you here, encouraging you to read on so you can find the closure you seek.

Now that we have made it so far in our journey of understanding and dealing with narcissists, we must understand the attraction between narcissists and codependents to realize how we end up embroiled in such toxic relationship dynamics. This relationship dynamic never works out because the codependent partner always realizes that their relationship is unhealthy. It does not satisfy their needs and desires as a person and as a partner. As in my case, the giver often ends up quitting the toxic relationship with a narcissist and comes to terms with the relationship dynamic that they had blindly fallen into. This pairing between a narcissist and a codependent rarely ever lasts, so why does it happen in the first place?

You see, narcissists and codependents are opposites, despite their underlying low self-esteem and vulnerabilities. Narcissists are high and mighty, with an inflated sense of self and a flagrant display of superiority. They cannot handle criticism and rejection of any kind. Any idea or thought that negates their authority or opinions is met with a violent and aggressive narcissistic rage.

On the other hand, a codependent person has trouble identifying and connecting with their own needs and desires. These people tend to prioritize the needs and desires of others above their own, and this is where the problem begins. They depend on other people for their emotional, mental, and spiritual fulfillment, and this dependence stems from their low self-esteem and vague self-identity. They have an inherent and overpowering desire to nurture, care for, and love others. In their quest and desire to please others and win over admiration, they cannot set boundaries to protect their emotional vulnerabilities.

Codependents associate great value and significance in serving others, helping people, and caring for people. They end up caring for and helping others at the cost of their emotional suffering and often sacrifice their mental well-being to keep the peace and avoid arguments that lead to disharmony. Their one genuine desire is to feel wanted and needed, for this desire fuels their staggeringly low self-esteem. When they feel unwanted and unneeded, they feel worthless and lose their will to live and be happy.

The pairing of a narcissist and a codependent is increasingly common, and we have all seen it around us. This relationship begins and works initially because both the narcissist and the codependent have a specific role to play, and they both enjoy playing it to a hilt!

The narcissist has no trouble or remorse for being the shining sun, and the codependent has little problem worshiping this sun and revolving around it. Narcissists believe that they cannot do anything wrong, and they are quite literally the best thing that could happen to the codependent. The narcissist associates great significance with their needs and desires, putting themselves over and above everyone and everything. At the same time, the codependent has an overwhelming desire to value the needs and desires of others above their own. The narcissist partner relies on the codependent to admire, praise, approve of them, and bolster their self-esteem. In contrast, the codependent partner obediently and passionately nurtures and serves their inflated ego.

The relationship between a narcissist and a codependent is toxic, manipulative, exploitative, abusive, and one-sided (Mayfield, 2020). It is based on an unequal distribution of power. The narcissist is always demanding and taking and depriving the codependent of everything, while the codependent is constantly nurturing, giving, and showering the narcissist with everything they have. Now, this is precisely the type of relationship that a narcissist yearns for, craves, and loves. Narcissists desire for nothing more than a person who places them high above on a pedestal, worshiping them and basking in their glory. Someone who can see them with the same adoration and admiration that they regard themselves as, of course, without seeing through the façade of their deep-rooted insecurities and shallow self-esteem.

As it happens, the relationship between a narcissist and a codependent isn't just unhealthy for the giver but also for the taker. It's a toxic relationship, and its harmful and damaging consequences impair the mental well-being of both partners. You see, these partners are constantly reinforcing each other's unhealthy traits and toxic habits, plying each other with the poison that worsens their conditions. A narcissist has no limits, and will go to all extents to manipulate, abuse, and exploit the codependent for their gains. The codependent will continue to give every ounce of their energy and love until they are empty inside. The narcissist is a hard to satisfy partner, and the codependent will work harder than ever to please the narcissist and win the approval they crave. The narcissist enjoys the efforts and the hard work the giver puts into a relationship and will exercise control, manipulation, and exploitative tactics to continue pushing the codependent to do more.

## UNDERSTANDING THE DIFFERENCES BETWEEN CODEPENDENCY AND NARCISSISM

On the one hand, we have narcissists with their inflated sense of entitlement, self-importance, and monstrous egos. On the other hand, we have codependents who are endlessly loyal martyrs and selfless lovers. So when we sit down to compare the differences between codependents and narcissists, we see two polar opposite personalities, right? Yet, interestingly, these two personalities have a great deal in common (Glass, 2020).

Let's take a look at some traits that narcissists share with codependents:

## Unconsciously Relying on Others

People with codependent and narcissistic personality traits struggle to form a self-image that serves as a mirror for every individual. This struggle to connect with their innate and true self leads them to create an idealized and fantasized self-image that they identify with and work hard to sustain. Naturally, this idealized self-image makes them unconsciously reliant and dependent on others for approval and validation. Narcissists are very inclined towards others, and they seek approval to validate and sustain their fragile sense of self and perpetually threatened ego. Their low self-esteem is fueled by the admiration, praise, and attention they receive from others. In most cases, narcissists and codependents acquire this unconscious need to depend on others from unhealthy or exploitative attachments formed during their childhood.

## Deep-rooted Guilt & Embarrassment

Both narcissists and codependents struggle with deep-rooted and internalized shame, guilt, and embarrassment that they carry since their early years. In addition, both personalities struggle with overpowering fear, anxieties, insecurities, and uncertainties they were exposed to as children. To cope with these unpleasant emotions and thoughts, codependents and narcissists give birth to an idealized and fantasized self-image.

Codependents create the image of a self-sacrificing martyr who dedicates their life for the affection, attention, and approval of others, willing to sacrifice their needs to satisfy others. In contrast, narcissists seek domination, power, and precedence over all others. Interestingly, when we look closely, we find that both these self-images stem from a deep-rooted sense of inferiority, embarrassment, and a fear of humiliation.

## Living in Perpetual Denial

Narcissists and codependents live in perpetual denial, eager to sustain their idealized self-image and fantasized realities. Codependents deny their own needs, desires, and emotions, and at times, even deny their need for codependency. They deny their desires by sacrificing their needs for others, all the while pretending that they don't need anything from anyone.

In contrast, narcissists deny their feelings in fear of revealing their vulnerabilities and weaknesses. They do not allow themselves to display any emotions that make them look weak or incapable of restraint. However, narcissists do not hold themselves back from exploding in rage, anger, and contempt.

## A Desire for Control

Narcissists and codependents desire to control others, directly or indirectly, to fuel and sustain their bliss and sense of self-worth. These two personalities manifest a wide array of controlling behaviors, such as lying, manipulation, exploitation, domination, and people-pleasing. The goal always revolves around garnering validation and applause to sustain their self-image.

Narcissists have a well-stocked arsenal of controlling tactics, emotionally exploitative strategies, and manipulative maneuvers, which they use as masterful tacticians to get precisely what they want from a person. Narcissists try to control everything, from their loved ones and colleagues to their environments and even their feelings.

## Inadequate Communication Skills

Codependents and narcissists are poor conversationalists with inadequate communication skills. They are unable to identify, process, and clearly explain their emotions. Narcissists struggle with communication on a much more profound level. They tend to cultivate dogmatic opinions, and their inflexible thinking makes them very demanding and overly critical of themselves and others. Deep down, both codependents and narcissists are unable to respect the feelings and dignity of others, and this lack of respect is the root cause for a wide array of communication troubles in any given relationship they attempt to cultivate with an average, healthy individual.

## THE CODEPENDENT NARCISSIST: WHERE DO NARCISSISM & CODEPENDENCY CONNECT?

After all the information we have processed, you must be wondering, can a narcissist also be codependent? Yes, both narcissists and codependents have overlapping traits. The narcissist yearns for applause, fame, and significance, while the codependent wants nothing more than to be desired and needed by someone. But at the core, both rely on others for dependence and validation to sustain their idealized self-image.

Narcissists have a much grander need to exert power over others and increase their narcissistic "supply" of praise, admiration, and attention.

Can codependents also harbor narcissistic traits? Answering this question is much more complex and requires us to dive deep into narcissists' manipulative and abusive tactics. In many cases, narcissists gaslight and manipulate their codependent partners into believing that they are the narcissists in the relationship, deflecting from all responsibility by shifting the blame.

However, this doesn't eliminate the possibility of code-pendents harboring narcissistic traits. Many of these traits stem from adverse childhood experiences, but codependents exhibit their narcissistic tendencies on infrequent occasions. It's hard to identify one consistent personality in individuals who exhibit both narcissistic and codependent traits. Now, let's drop the big question.

**What Is a Codependent Narcissist?**

Narcissists cover their vulnerabilities, emotional wounds, fragile ego, and deeply hurt core with carefully concocted layers of self-importance, exaggerated superiority, and a haughty demeanor. In their minds, they have evolved so far away from their faithful and innate self-image that the only way they can maintain and sustain their idealized self-image is by manipulating and exploiting others to remain reliant on them. But deep down, narcissists are the ones who are reliant on others to sustain their idealized sense of self-worth. Being left alone scares them because it would deprive them of the audience they need to feel admired, cherished, applauded, and respected (Glass, 2020).

Narcissists who harbor codependent traits have an insatiable desire to feel loved, feared, praised, or respected by others.

## THE ATTACHMENT STYLES OF A NARCISSIST

Did you know that our personalities are shaped, cultivated, and carved by the relationships we harbor with our loved ones, starting from our earliest childhood relationships? The personality traits and attachment styles of narcissists, like everyone else, are also shaped during childhood (Glass, 2020).

In terms of their attachment styles, we must identify two broad types of narcissistic personalities:

1. Grandiose Narcissists
2. Vulnerable Narcissists

Much as the name implies, grandiose narcissists are brimming with arrogance and an inflated sense of entitlement. They envelop their personalities with a false aura of independence and self-sufficiency. These narcissists learn to avoid attachment since their childhood years, and their relationships are damaged by their tendency to avoid intimacy and steer clear of all commitments and responsibilities. They act self-obsessed and make others think they don't need anyone to stay happy and fulfilled.

In contrast, vulnerable narcissists exhibit overwhelming anxiety in all their relationships and attachments. They strive for reassurances from their partners and loved ones to feel secure, admired, and loved.

# PART II

## DEALING WITH THE NARCISSISTS WHO YOU CAN'T ESCAPE

Not everyone has the courage, emotional strength, or even the luxury of walking out from an abusive relationship and carving out the life they desire to maintain their emotional well-being and mental peace. Unfortunately, even those who manage to take the giant leap of eliminating the unavoidable narcissists in their lives find themselves constantly being cornered and drawn into battle by the narcissist who refuses to let them be at peace.

When you can't escape a narcissist, you must play and beat them at their own game. This endeavor requires a formidable strategy to shift the balance of power and give you the upper hand when dealing with a narcissist. In the second part of this book, we will focus on equipping ourselves with strategies, tactics, and solutions to deal with a narcissist when leaving or going 'no contact' are not viable options.

In this section, we will acknowledge all the narcissists in our lives. For some, the narcissist is perhaps a sibling, parent, or coworker who seems to have embarked on a mission to sabotage their careers. For others, the narcissist may be a spouse or an ex-spouse they now must co-parent with to maintain a safe and healthy environment for their children.

We will look at a wide array of techniques, tactics, and solutions, and with each chapter, we will explore strategies to help you reclaim your power and find your balance. But before we dive deeper into these strategies, I must introduce you to a discovery that has proven life-changing for me: the grey rock method.

As a universal technique of responding to manipulative behavior and dealing with narcissists, the grey rock method will serve as our light as we navigate coping strategies with the unavoidable narcissist.

## DECODING THE GREY ROCK METHOD

What comes to your mind when you picture a grey rock? Here's what we usually think: an unappealing and common rock that fails to impress the onlookers with its ordinary features. In the psychological realm, the grey rock method aims to achieve just that: rock-like unresponsiveness and a refusal to interact and engage with abusive and manipulative behavior (Caporuscio, 2021).

The goal is to go by unnoticed, and while you can't transform yourself into a rock, you can put up a sturdy wall of rocks to block out all abuse and manipulation. The grey rock method, a universal technique, is highly useful in dealing with toxic people and those diagnosed with narcissistic personality disorder.

Interestingly, this technique doesn't demand much on your part. All you must do is be the dullest, most lackluster, and uninspiring version of yourself while dealing with a narcissist. Remember, narcissists and manipulators thrive on drama. Dramatic emotions are their supply, and when you switch to being dull and uninteresting, you deny them the supply they so anxiously crave. Acting bland, boring, and tedious will sabotage all their efforts to exploit and dominate you.

It may seem easy but putting this technique to use is a bit complicated. Therefore, it's essential to know when to use this strategy and when to avoid it. When dealing with narcissists, any method can backfire easily when met with the infamous narcissistic rage. Of course, cutting off narcissists and toxic people is essential and a manifestation of self-love, but what if you have to co-parent with a narcissist or survive daily interactions and collaborations at work?

Grey rocking will come to your rescue by making you so dull and boring that the narcissist wouldn't feel encouraged or interested enough to manipulate you. Non-stimulating conversations and lackluster meetings will discourage them from meeting you and interacting with you because narcissists want drama above all else. They thrive on chaos and conflict, for it gives them the thrill of evoking a roller-coaster of unpleasant emotions in others. Deny them this thrill by offering nothing in response. Don't share your anger, contempt, and rage, or even your happiness, smiles, or salutations. Instead, make yourself wholly disengaged and unappealing, and avoid answering their questions with comprehensive responses (Raypole, 2019).

Ideally, mastering an unresponsive poker face will have narcissists rolling in internal discomfort, perplexed by your lack of responsiveness. Vague responses and indifference can drive a narcissist crazy by denying them the fuel they need to manipulate and exploit you.

Essentially, the grey rock method is all about disconnecting and disengaging with narcissists and toxic people. Even eye contact should be avoided to disengage entirely and break off all emotional ties to send a powerful message of detachment. Narcissists thrive on attention, and when you withhold your attention, you send a clear statement of refusal to give them what they desire. Disengaging won't be easy, for the narcissist will try everything, from cruelty to sentimental ploys, to gain your sympathy and elicit a response from you. Deny them this pleasure by redirecting your attention to any activity or individual who helps you feel distracted and disconnected from manipulation.

Focus on keeping all your conversations and interactions as short as possible. Don't get into debates or long discussions and make it evident that you're uninterested in prolonging the interaction more than necessary. Limiting your responses to yes or no is an excellent strategy to maintain a tight-lipped demeanor that will discourage them from probing you further.

No matter what you do, never tell the narcissist that you are intentionally blocking them out and disengaging them. Narcissists are master manipulators and will quickly catch onto your technique, but if you tell them that you're grey rocking them, you will lose the power you are trying to reclaim. Remember, the goal is to make yourself uninteresting, so the narcissist willingly decides to leave you alone. You don't want to anger them or put up a fight because the drama and chaos stemming from this situation will make them feel powerful and ecstatic enough to attack you from a vantage point that makes you feel secure.

With a strategy like grey rocking that encourages disengaging and disconnecting, it's hard to stay focused on your true self and avoid such behaviors from permeating all your relationships and communications. Finding your balance is critical, and luckily, disengaging with the narcissist in your life is the right step to reclaim emotional balance and power.

## Want to Help Another Survivor?
## Pay It Forward

How did *you* come to realize you were dealing with a narcissist?

If you are anything like me, you knew something wasn't quite right, but you didn't know exactly *what* you were experiencing. Does that sound familiar?

It wasn't until I tearfully poured out my heart to my therapist, who identified my husband as a narcissist, that I was given a starting point in my research. The more I read, the more I wasn't as alone in my pain. I realized I didn't imagine things. *I wasn't going crazy.*

I hope that as you finish reading the first half of this book, you are already feeling validated, empowered, and not as alone as when you first started reading.

Would you like to pass this empowerment on to others? I imagine survivors suffering the same emotions I had when I began my healing journey - confused, desperate for answers, feeling alone, and impossibly stuck.

If you find this book valuable so far, would you consider taking a brief moment to leave an honest review? Your review might give one more survivor the courage to take life-changing action in their circumstances. Your review might help one more survivor stop allowing abuse from a narcissist. Your review just might enable a survivor to reclaim their sense of self. Before going any further, I hope that you will take a short break to leave a review or rating of this book before continuing - it will take less than a minute. (For your convenience, you may scan the QR code below to leave your review.)

Lastly, if you know of any other survivors who might benefit from this book, I hope you will tell them about how it has helped you.

Now, let's dive back into the book and strategize how you can deal with the specific narcissistic relationships in your life.

To your continued healing,

Sydney

# 4

# NARCISSISM IN THE FAMILY

Living with a narcissist in your immediate family is a lifelong journey of turmoil, chaos, and processing unpleasant emotions that shatter your self-esteem and self-worth. Living with a narcissist can cast an overwhelmingly burdensome strain on our energy levels, leaving us feeling drained and empty as we struggle to soothe and appease the narcissist. When our most dedicated and devoted efforts fail to make them happy or grateful, we start realizing our relationship dynamics' oddness and unhealthy elements. A narcissist always seizes the upper hand and rejoicing in power.

Strategies and coping methods of dealing with a narcissistic family member depend entirely on who this family member is—is it a distant relative, like a cousin, an aunt, or a grandparent? In that case, breaking off the relationship and going no contact is an easy and livable choice.

However, if the narcissist is your parent or a sibling, breaking off all communication is not an option. So, what should you do?

First, we must explore the relationship dynamics of two narcissists in the family: siblings and parents. And then, we will revisit these relationships with practical strategies and coping techniques.

## IDENTIFYING PATTERNS IN THE NARCISSISTIC FAMILY

Growing up in a narcissistic family turns childhood experiences into a never-ending struggle for survival. The narcissistic family dynamics deny all opportunities to learn how to share and coexist while cultivating your own identity and a strong personality. Instead, life becomes a constant fight to protect your mental well-being and your self-esteem. As a result, children born to narcissistic parents seldom have healthy childhood experiences. Instead, their life trajectory revolves around finding their role or their position within the family. In a healthy family, every family member has a designation and is celebrated for their talents and strengths and helped to overcome their weaknesses or mistakes. However, in narcissistic families, children often struggle to find and connect with their true selves because they are pawns and pieces on a chessboard for their narcissist parent (Dodgson, 2020).

All family members and children must comply with the dynamics or gameplay the narcissist parent wishes to create within their family. Every child is a piece on a chessboard that the narc parent can use to serve a purpose. Each piece must move and serve its purpose precisely as planned by the narc, and at times, one child can be used to attack the other child in a manipulative game created by the parent to exert their power and dominance over the family. All these rules and unquestioned obedience give birth to unhealthy family dynamics. All family members, especially children, are constantly living in survival mode, anxious to avoid their parent's narcissistic rage. As a result, children either support the narcissist parent or become the object of their narcissistic rage and contempt.

The parenting style of a narcissist is somewhat similar to a chessboard, and they dominate the gameplay, making erratic decisions by favoring one child and exposing the other to their hostility and wrath. These manipulative games and toxic parenting styles give birth to five family patterns as identified by Shannon Thomas, a renowned trauma therapist (Dodgson, 2020).

Let's take a closer look at these patterns:

## 1. The Neutral Sibling

The neutral sibling must tread a careful path that is akin to walking on eggshells in their quest of maintaining a balance between appeasing their narcissistic parent and staying loyal to their siblings. Essentially, they play the role of a peacemaker—a role that requires perpetual aerobics of their emotions and cognitive capabilities in their struggle to keep the peace. Being a neutral sibling isn't easy because, to act like the glue holding the whole family together, one has to unsee and unhear many things.

The mediator and peacemaker never achieve any peace or tranquility in life, for this role requires them to silence their conscience to keep the peace. It's an unhealthy and toxic role to play, for they find themselves forced to deny everything they see and hear just to appease everyone and keep the peace. Moreover, due to their peacemaking efforts and denial of the truth, the neutral one constantly struggles to establish a deep connection with other siblings.

The neutral one survives by erecting a giant, emotional wall around them to tune out all the pain and trauma and focus on their quest to keep everyone happy and maintain a peaceful environment at home. The neutral sibling is constantly in denial to maintain the façade of a happy and healthy home. They remain fixated on the healthy elements that make their family functional and happy.

### 2. The Needy Sibling

Much as the name implies, the needy sibling has an excessive need to rely and depend on others. This sibling either needs to rely on their parents or harbor narcissistic traits that make them overly dependent and needy. Thomas explains that narcissistic parents tend to "infantilize" the needy one and intentionally curb them from becoming independent and self-sufficient adults. This infantilizing allows the narc parent to keep enjoying their narcissistic supply of dependence, admiration, and love.

More importantly, showering one child with love, care and compassion allows the narc parent a clean chit to deny any injustices they have committed towards other family members. Suppose they have harmed other children emotionally or physically. In that case, they will quickly point towards the needy sibling as a shining example of this parental love and compassion to counterbalance any kind of judgment or criticism of their parenting style. You see, the narcissistic parent doesn't want that sibling ever to become strong enough to get independent and self-sufficient, regardless of their lofty claims, because they want to enable a dependency to bolster their self-esteem.

As we explore this pattern, we must understand that in some cases, the needy sibling can also harbor toxic tendencies and manufactured dependency. Thomas explains that the relationship between a narcissistic parent and sibling is much like a "toxic dance" that triggers an imbalance between siblings, giving rise to competition, envy, and utter chaos.

### 3. The Flying Monkey

All narcissistic families have one "flying monkey" —the sibling involved in cornering everyone and creating chaos by deepening the rifts and making everyone upset. The flying monkey is a toxic embodiment of their narcissistic parents, and they enjoy harassing other family members. These siblings learn the games their narcissistic parents play and are inspired by these games. They start learning and developing toxic behaviors of their own. The flying monkey sibling also has an unwavering allegiance to the narcissistic parent, and they reinforce this allegiance by acting as accomplices in the abuse meted out towards other siblings.

The flying monkey, a reference Thomas has captured from the Wizard of Oz, reports everything the siblings say about the narc parent, acting as the eyes and ears of the narcissist. But despite all their dedication and unwavering allegiance, even the flying monkey, like all others, remain unsafe from the narcissistic rage and wrath. Then, somewhere down the road, after alienating and abusing all other siblings in cahoots with the narcissistic parent, the flying monkey ends up becoming the target of the narcissist's wrath. The flying monkey must never stop feeding the parent their narcissistic supply of admiration and allegiance, rendering them unable to build a life for themselves.

At some point, the flying monkey will wake up from this trance and muster the free will to choose to continue feeding the narcissistic supply or leave and carve out their journey towards adulthood, success, and happiness. But make no mistake, the flying monkey understands their choices and performs the bidding of their narcissistic parent with full knowledge that such behaviors should not be tolerated or excused. And yet, they continue to fuel the fire by adding more gasoline rather than leaving and questioning the toxicity of the narcissistic parent.

## 4. The Withdrawn Sibling

It's easy to confuse the withdrawn sibling with the neutral one, but the two are poles apart. The withdrawn sibling is a keen and ardent observer, absorbing everything like a sponge and understanding the reality of everything rolling out around them. These siblings have a deep-rooted coping mechanism that alerts them to run for cover and secure themselves. Most of the time, the withdrawn siblings keep to themselves and focus on flying under the radar—a strategy that doesn't always work.

Through all the manipulative tactics, they see the emotional cues, games, and chaos intentionally created by their narcissistic parent. They refuse to buy into the lies, and in most cases, the withdrawn sibling is the one who speaks up about the toxic family dynamics and abusive tactics of the narcissist parent. And needless to say, their willingness to speak out against the narc quickly transforms them into the "scapegoated" child. The scapegoat child becomes the target of all the abuse and toxicity a narcissistic parent can channel. They also end up being abused by the flying monkeys in the family. Because of their vocalness about discussing the toxicity and wrong in their family, the withdrawn sibling often ends up standing alone in the line of fire.

## 5. Pseudomutuality

For an outsider who doesn't understand the inner dynamics, a narcissistic family looks perfectly healthy and happy. But when one starts peeling at the fragmented and shaky surface, one finds a deeply segregated family and broken to the point of dysfunctionality. Thomas uses the clinical term "pseudomutuality" to describe the fake intimacy and closeness within a family.

Pseudomutuality, a false sense of intimacy, is the glue that keeps a narcissistic family together, hiding away all the toxic dynamics responsible for adverse childhood experiences of all children born to narcissistic parents. Unfortunately, for someone entering such a poisonous family unit after marrying the narcissist's children, understanding and embracing these unhealthy dynamics is a long and arduous struggle.

## COPING WITH A NARCISSISTIC PARENT

There are hundreds and thousands of people who walk the earth with the heavy emotional burden of their trauma from their narcissistic parent and the pain of adverse childhood experiences. There's nothing worse than living and struggling with a narcissistic parent, for parents must embody everything loving and caring about this world to create a safe and secure mental model for their children. Parents must shower their children with unconditional love and support, dealing with their mistakes in a positive manner to give them a secure and loving childhood. But growing up with a narcissistic parent denies a normal childhood, as children are constantly embroiled in a struggle to rescue their self-esteem and find security and safety. Amid all the manipulative games, narcissistic rage, and chessboard tactics, children end up losing their innocence, sense of self-worth, sense of security, confidence, and strength.

Being raised by a narcissist encourages the belief of not being "good enough"—an idea that most children carry into adulthood and end up embarking on a lifetime of people-pleasing and appeasing others to feel secure in their love (Caprino, 2016). What's worse is that living with a narcissistic parent damages all emotional boundaries, dismantling the barriers and systems that regulate information and contact between you and the outside world. These dismantled boundaries render the child with numerous communication and coordination defects, and they struggle to communicate with confidence and courage.

They grow up as exceedingly insecure adults with a fragmented sense of self, which thwarts their ability to form intimate relationships or succeed at work. As a result, many adult children born to narcissists struggle to carve out success in their personal and professional relationships. But the real tragedy is the fact that very few children manage to heal and recover from the trauma because they don't realize that their childhood was destructive, toxic, and unhealthy. Moreover, given the esteemed position of parents in all religions and cultures, these children struggle to find clarity and understand the role played by the narcissistic parent in their adverse childhood experiences.

Being raised by a narcissist creates numerous disadvantages for children, the primary being the lack of boundaries one needs to maintain to feel confident, courageous, and healthy. My research and exploration into the lives of children born to narcissists revealed that many adult children end up spending their entire lives believing they are not "good enough" to enjoy any kind of happiness, love, or admiration (Caprino 2016). These adult children constantly seek validation and approval, and yet, they always feel unsatisfied with their self-image.

Most children of narcissists are profoundly insecure and increasingly sensitive, and they struggle to imagine themselves as lovable people who are worthy of success, admiration, or even love. Unfortunately, these traits are very similar to those of narcissists, and that's because of a lifelong struggle with their parent's constant need for admiration and devotion. Adult children born to narcissists firmly believe that love is always conditional, as reinforced by the brand of love demonstrated by their narc parent. They think that they will have to meet certain conditions and demands or perform specific actions to secure the love they desire.

## OUTLINING THE CHARACTERISTICS OF A NARCISSISTIC PARENT

Narcissistic parents are overly possessive and try to foster a dependency because they regard their children as an extension of themselves and the primary source to satisfy their insatiable need for the narcissistic supply of obedience, respect, adoration, and admiration. For them, their children are objects to show off and win applause. A typical narcissistic parent would boast about the talents and capabilities of their child to show what a fantastic job they've done, only to embarrass, humiliate, and manipulate their children in private. You see, their children are nothing more than pawns on a chessboard or an object to capture the attention of others.

Children quickly learn to find their existence within the molds their narcissistic parent has created for them to fit into, and this gives rise to unbelievable anxiety, stress, and trauma for a child who is struggling to carve out an individualistic personality, or even the child who is subduing their true nature to appease their narc parent. So you see, narcissistic parents have a carefully planned schedule for their children to maintain stability in their lives, and the children must embrace this plan wholeheartedly.

The problems arise when the child starts voicing their thoughts and asserting their own beliefs, triggering contempt, anger, and punishment from the narc parent. This process invalidates the feelings and emotions of the child, making the children feel insignificant and unvalued.

As a result, children subconsciously learn to associate little value with their feelings and end up drowning their desires to maintain a peaceful environment at home.

Mind you, narcissistic parents aren't always cruel and obsessive. At times, they can be overwhelmingly kind, but this kindness almost always comes with a hefty price. Children quickly realize that the kindness and compassion of their narcissistic parents make them indebted to their parents. The dynamics revolve around "I did this for you, now you must do this for me" for little acts of parental love and care. So, the child learns that love, respect, and kindness are conditional and a debt that must be repaid.

Here are some common characteristics to help you identify a narcissistic parent (Launder, n.d.):

- Selfish, childlike, and immature behavior.
- The need to monopolize every conversation and make it about themselves.
- Bragging about your talents and achievements to others, but denying you any kind of acknowledgment, validation, or emotional support in private.
- Controlling, dominative, and aggressive in private, and amicable and loving in front of others.
- Making you feel horrible and humiliated when you fail to do something they want you to do immediately.

- Tendency to blame others for any issues you're experiencing because of their actions or neglect.
- Inducing guilt by reminding you of all the things they have done for you.
- Damaging your self-esteem with harsh and negative opinions at home and putting up a supportive front in public.
- A ruthless and aggressive need to stay on top and dominate everything.
- Extremely unforgiving when their demands are not fulfilled.
- Induces anxiety and says hurtful things to reduce your confidence and self-esteem.

Narcissistic parents are rashly unpredictable, which makes the entire childhood experience overwhelmingly traumatic and deeply unsettling. Little children are dependents who cannot leave their parent's home, which leaves little choice but to embrace the humiliation and sacrifice their self-esteem to win over their narc parent's affection. Most children blame themselves and suffer unbelievable trauma by internalizing the fact that they are the underlying problem behind the lack of affection, empathy, and care exhibited by their narcissistic parents. Narcissistic parents further fuel this insecurity and deep-rooted guilt in their children by constantly reinforcing the belief that they are perfect parents. Any negativity or difficulty they suffered was because of their child.

What is the biggest struggle of growing up under the care of a narcissistic parent? The struggle of realizing the trauma and pain they experienced as children. Our families serve as the primary educators. We only learn what they expose us to, so it can take years for adult children to realize their narcissistic parents' odd and unhealthy parenting styles.

## LIVING WITH A NARCISSISTIC PARENT: IMPACT ON YOUR MENTAL HEALTH

If you've grown up with a narcissistic parent and understand their condition, you can understand the adverse impact of the generational trauma on your mental and physical health. However, if you're still struggling to realize why your parent behaved in such an odd and unhealthy way, you're still trying to understand what went wrong and how it impacted you on a deeper, emotional level. Some say the psychological scars of living with a narcissistic parent never truly heal. In contrast, others say that with dedicated efforts and continued therapy, the debilitating effects of adverse childhood experiences start diminishing if not disappearing altogether.

It's hard to process and understand these parents, for they are two different people. In public, they become the perfect embodiment of the loving, doting, and caring parents, and at home, behind closed doors, the monster is unleashed. As a result, children find themselves exposed to the terror of narcissistic rage, contempt, and humiliation. For a child, the confusion created by this double-sided personality challenges their sense of reality. Gradually, children lose trust in their memories and cognition, and this confusion becomes a permanent aspect of their character.

Narcissistic parents are control freaks and overly possessive. They wish to live life vicariously through their children, and for this purpose, they ignore the dreams and desires of their children and map out a trajectory for them to follow without making the slightest of changes. They want their will to be carried out like gospel, and children end up learning that their needs, desires, and goals are of little significance. The narcissist's child is constantly struggling and striving to become the perfect child and live up to the unrealistic standards and insatiable demands of their perpetually unsatisfied parent. The inability to make the narcissist happy gives rise to depression and anxiety in the child.

**Traits of Adult Children of a Narcissistic Parent**

Parenting styles have a profound impact on a child's mental and character development and personality traits. Let's take a closer look at the characteristics of adult children of a narcissistic parent (Thomas, 2021).

They include:

- Struggle with guilt.
- Indecision and difficulty making choices.

- Internalized gaslighting and a tendency to deny their own feelings/needs.
- Difficulty setting boundaries and rationalizing love and loyalty.
- Overpowering resilience and emotional strength.
- Chronic habit to self-blame.
- Echoism.
- Insecure attachment style.
- Parentified child.

For children, such an unhealthy parenting style makes the parent increasingly unpredictable, erratic, and unreliable. Little ones struggle to understand how to win over their parents' love and admiration. It leads to a lifetime of walking on eggshells because they live with the over-whelming responsibility to make their parents happy and content. Children also quickly learn that the love and kindness of their parent come at a cost, and this cost is often paid with deep humiliation and by sacrificing their self-esteem, confidence, and desires.

When I look back to my relationship with my husband and his relationship with our children as a narcissistic parent, I remember the fear, trauma, and anxiety my boys experienced and the joy of being liberated from that fear when we finally decided to leave. When my husband would be at work, my sons and I would enjoy the carefree environment of our home. If one of my sons accidentally spilled something, no one would make a big deal about it, and we would clean it up without a word of humiliation.

However, if such an accident were to happen in front of my husband, he wouldn't waste a second to launch into a hurtful tirade about my son's carelessness. At the time, all my children were less than ten years old, and little ones don't need such aggressive and harsh reprimanding over minor accidents that happen because of kids just being kids. The level of discipline or criticism he exposed them to never actually matched their mistakes.

When we eventually left my husband, the boys and I could finally live our lives without any semblance of fear corroding our minds. We were free, once and for all, and as time passed, we saw dramatic improvements in our mental and physical well-being. For myself, the nagging depression and anxiety were gone, and over time, my heart palpitations subsided, and I felt rejuvenated. One day, as I was sitting with my eldest son, I casually asked him how he felt about living in our new apartment, tiny in comparison to the home we left, and he calmly responded, "I love it here. I don't get yelled at for dumb things." I couldn't have said it better myself.

Much like we discussed in the family patterns of narcissistic families, my husband had also assigned specific roles with each of my sons. My eldest son was a punching bag for my husband's emotional abuse, and as a teenager, he was diagnosed with depression, anxiety, and PTSD. I assumed that these symptoms stemmed from the trauma of my husband's suicide, but his doctor corrected me by explaining that these conditions stemmed from the abuse he suffered at the hands of my husband's narcissistic rage.

Unfortunately, my eldest son has once overheard my husband tell his sister (my son's aunt), ". . . Only seven more years, and I don't have to deal with him (my son) anymore." My son was 11 at the time, and the sense of abandonment was crushing.

My middle son was the scapegoat, and he was ridiculed and teased regularly. My husband could never relate with him, so instead of focusing on connecting with him, he just pushed him away with his dismissive behavior. My second son learned just to lie low and try not to upset my husband.

My youngest son was the golden child because my husband could easily identify with him, and he showered our youngest one with special treatment, which is why, to this day, he doesn't fully comprehend the abuse and trauma the rest of the family has suffered.

On infrequent "good days," my husband was fun and joyful to be around. He would delight us with the best chocolate milkshakes and mango lassis, chase the boys around the house with their Nerf guns, and play with their Lego sets. Unfortunately, most days weren't like this because my husband played and engaged with the kids only when convenient for him. We had to tip-toe around his mood swings. I couldn't help but notice the jealousy my husband felt and expressed towards our children. Later, my research introduced me to the fact that narcs are known to be jealous of their kids. I noticed that my husband's narcissistic tendencies increased whenever the boys needed more attention from me. And these tendencies heightened and grew with the birth of each child. I only came to this realization in hindsight.

## TECHNIQUES & STRATEGIES OF DEALING WITH A NARCISSISTIC PARENT

It's hard to push our parents out of our lives. Try as we might, deep down, we want them to be a part of our lives and support us emotionally and physically. But one must be firm and rational when dealing with a narcissistic parent.

Here are some strategies that will help you immensely (Galperin, n.d.):

**Build Awareness**

The first step is to realize what is happening to you isn't normal or healthy and build your awareness and understanding by devouring scientific literature and psychological research on narcissistic traits and tendencies. This research and awareness will help you understand their behavior and drain out the emotional trauma. Understanding their condition will make it easier for you not to feel hurt and targeted by their abuse.

**Let It All Go**

Once you understand the psychological dynamics of narcissistic disorder, it's time to accept and let it all go. Don't let your narcissistic parent's emotional disturbances and generational trauma reflect your emotional well-being and quality of life. It's simple: accept their personality traits and let them go because you can't help them fix things unless they make an effort.

## Don't Let Yourself Be Gaslighted

Resisting gaslighting attempts from narcissistic parents is the hardest part of dealing with them. Still, once you accept their personality traits, you realize that you're dealing with an unempathetic person who doesn't acknowledge your emotional trauma and concerns. Don't allow yourself to be gaslighted by simply taking away their power to invalidate your emotions. In this technique, the grey rock method will help you immensely.

## Be Compassionate

The choice to be compassionate and empathetic is genuinely yours, and it's a powerful decision to make. Being compassionate while respecting healthy boundaries, empathetic, and caring will bring you up with resilience and courage, giving you a chance to fight the trauma and abuse with kindness.

## Prioritize Self-Love

Loving yourself is truly the most powerful and courageous technique to deal with the abuse of a narcissistic parent. Parents are supposed to love their children unconditionally, but you will have to do their job for them when your parent is a narcissist. Love yourself endlessly, and if self-love demands that you put distance between yourself and your narc parent, then that's the right decision to make!

## Find Support

Having a social circle of support from family, friends, and loved ones will give you the shoulders to lean on and unpack the burdens you're carrying. Having friends and loved ones who understand your pain and wish to protect you from trauma can make a world of difference to one's life and well-being.

## Reclaim Your Confidence

For years, your narc parent has attacked your self-esteem, depriving you of confidence and self-assuredness. Now, it's time to reclaim all the power you have lost. Start building your confidence by pursuing your passions and dreams, setting achievable milestones, and basking in recognition of your wins and successes.

## Setting Boundaries

Setting boundaries with narcissists isn't an easy endeavor, but once you manage to assert some boundaries, the equation becomes more balanced. Suddenly, narcissists lose all power over you because they have to play by your rules or risk being ousted from the game. Setting boundaries will deter them from the threat of consequences, and the rules will help you escape the narcissistic rage, forcing them to play nice.

## Understanding Your Experiences

It's essential to recount your experiences of narcissistic rage and abuse in the light of the scientific and medical research you explore. Make a journal devoted to dealing with your traumatic memories and experiences and write it all down so you feel lighter and released. Once you've written down everything, this journal will help you overcome traumatic memories by reminding yourself that it wasn't your fault, and you didn't deserve the abuse you suffered.

## Don't Deny Your Grief

The loss of one's childhood, the trauma of an absent parent, and the struggle of having to appease your parent to win over their love is an unprecedented and unbelievable amount of torture. Don't hold back from grieving. You're bound to feel jealous and deprived when you see parents sharing love with their children. So, allow yourself moments of grief so you can let it all out and begin anew with a positive state of mind.

## COPING WITH A NARCISSISTIC SIBLING

Understanding and embracing the narcissistic traits of a sibling will help you feel empowered and in control of the relationship and overall family dynamics. Empathetic siblings often struggle because of the sibling who ends up taking all the attention and denies you grace and respect, shattering your sense of self-esteem. However, knowledge about their condition will help you heal and make decisions to protect yourself from emotional abuse and manipulation.

Here are some common traits of narcissistic siblings (@dealwithnarcissist, 2020):

- Always craving and plotting to become the center of attention.
- An uncontrollable and insatiable thirst for approval, praise, and attention.
- A chronic habit of comparing themselves with others.
- Intense jealousy and competitiveness.
- An inflated sense of entitlement; acting as if you owe them an enormous debt.
- Lack of empathy and emotional recognition.
- A constant desire to talk about themselves and monopolize conversations.
- Inability to respect your boundaries.
- Constantly plotting to take advantage of you and manipulate you.
- An exaggerated belief of being unique.
- Inability to accept criticism, blame, constructive feedback, or responsibility.

The underlying traits, such as a lack of empathy, entitlement, superiority, jealousy, and competitiveness, tend to be the same in all narcissists. However, relationships are a clear-cut defining factor because they establish the context of your proximity and connection with the narcissist. Living with a narcissistic sibling isn't easy because they feel far more superior and important than you. They constantly strive to claim and retain their supposedly rightful position as the family genius, success story, and powerhouse of talents and goodness. Family dinners and get-togethers are filled with jokes that make them look brighter and superior and leave you feeling belittled and embarrassed. Since they imagine themselves as the superior child, they feel entitled to get everything they desire, from their parent's attention and adoration to the best in education, career, love and marriage, and even children. However, they create disturbances for their siblings because they feel entitled to their sibling's love, money, help, and loyalty. Narcissistic siblings can parasitically live off others without an ounce of gratitude or appreciation, and you may have felt victimized and exploited by these behaviors.

Does your narcissistic sibling show a blatant unwillingness to recognize your trauma and troubles and respect your feelings and desires? Narcissistic siblings are unempathetic and incapable of acknowledging the harm they have caused others. They don't have the time or patience to listen to your problems, but you have no choice but to listen to them complain about their issues for hours.

How does one deal with such toxic, manipulative, and exploitative behavior? Recap to the grey rock method, one doesn't deal with it at all. Becoming an unresponsive grey rock is your best and safest bet to end all their narcissistic drama and attention-grabbing behaviors.

Here are some other tricks that will help you deal with narcissistic siblings (*Narcissistic Brother and Sister Sibling Traits*, n.d.):

- Don't share your thoughts and knowledge about their narcissistic tendencies and disorder with them. It would only trigger them, and before you know it, they will embark on a toxic agenda to annihilate you, or at least dismantle your relationship and reputation in front of the rest of the family. Narcissists are pathological liars who will go to significant limits to make themselves look good and make you look hideously bad.
- Don't waste your energies by engaging with them, emotionally or verbally. Instead, protect and preserve your energies, and focus them on activities, projects, and decisions that reward you mentally, physically, socially, or financially.
- Start trusting your intuition when it sends you warning signals about the narc's true intentions and behaviors. Don't try to rationalize their toxic behaviors by empathizing with their "struggles" or making excuses out of loyalty. Your empathy should be your strength, not your weakness.
- Build your knowledge about narcissism and narcissistic traits, and make a habit of writing down your experiences so you can ponder over

them while learning more and exploring the experiences of other victims of narcissistic abuse.

- Accepting and rationalizing the truth is a painful yet necessary process. Understanding their condition will give you a world of closure, and you will feel the weight lifting off you.
- Last but most certainly not least, be sure to set some hard and firm boundaries to restrict your relationship with a narcissistic sibling. Don't allow them to walk in at their leisure and wreak havoc in your life without an ounce of remorse or acceptance. Setting boundaries will help limit your interactions and heartbreak.

# 5

# NARCISSISM IN THE WORKPLACE

M odern businesses and organizations operate in increasingly diverse workplace settings and cultures. Diversity allows us to experience the beauty of other personalities, cultures, and ethnicities, but it also exposes us to a broad spectrum of personality disorders and toxic traits. People from all kinds of backgrounds, adverse childhood experiences, and dealing with them in a strictly formal and hierarchical workplace environment can get extremely challenging.

Pop culture and cinematic depictions of psychological disorders often paint patients as helpless and incapacitated. While that is true for most people struggling with mental illnesses, it is often not true in NPD and psychopathic behaviors. Renowned British journalist Job Ronson, an avid and credible criminal profiler, immersed himself in criminal profiling in light of psychological diagnosis and research. In his book, *The Psychopath Test*, he claimed that his study revealed a correlation between psychopathy and people working in powerful and influential executive positions (Bagai, n.d.). Ronson said that psychopathy traits are four times higher in influential executives and corporate bigwigs than in the general population. Chiefs, executives, CEOs, managers, and bosses are likely to harbor narcissistic traits. That's right, your boss could be a narc, and we are about to decode how you can best deal with them in the workplace productively without jeopardizing your career.

## SPOTTING A NARCISSIST IN THE WORKPLACE

We've already discussed the underlying traits and symptoms to help you identify narcissistic behavior. Now, we will examine how narcissistic behavior manifests itself in the workplace.

Here are some common signs of workplace narcissism (Plato's Stunt Double, 2020):

### Mobbing

Mobbing is another word for a heightened form of bullying where a group of bullies targets an individual instead of one bully. Naturally, the narcissist is the ringleader of this mob, exploiting, coercing, and encouraging them to prey on your vulnerabilities and bully you into submission. Overt narcissists or extroverted ring leaders are likely to join in on the bullying. In contrast, vulnerable or introverted narcissists are likely to sit back and watch the show after manipulating and coercing other members into bullying their target. Keep in mind that introverted narcissists are far more dangerous than their extroverted counterparts because they put an enormous amount of energy into planning and plotting, setting the stage for your humiliation.

## Taking Credit for Someone Else's Hard Work

Narcissists bask in the attention and recognition they receive for their talents and hard work—even if it isn't their talent and hard work that's being praised. They don't care much about professional integrity and courtesy. All they want is to be the person standing in the face of glory and applause. As a result, they can be highly unscrupulous at times, taking all the credit for their subordinates' hard work and dedication—sometimes even ending up over-shadowing the contributions of entire teams.

## Backhanded and Forced Compliments

Narcissists simply cannot come to terms with the fact that someone is more talented, successful, and gifted than them. If they see someone who can compete with their talents, or heaven forbid, do better than them, they will be engulfed with fury, envy, and frustration. This explains why narcissists are not generous at giving compliments, but rather, it's tough for them to praise someone unless they want to exploit or manipulate that someone. A narcissistic boss, manager, or colleague will greet your success with forced, backhanded compliments, fuming inwardly with narcissistic rage that they are too careful to let out.

## A Penchant for Ridiculing & Humiliating Others

Narcissists are drowning with shame, guilt, insecurities, and the fear of their incapabilities, which explains why they ridicule, shame, and humiliate others to feel good about themselves. For example, does your narcissistic boss or coworker ridicule you in front of your coworkers and team members? That's a common sign of workplace narcissism, and you can be sure that your ridicule is fueling the narc's monstrous ego with waves of satisfaction.

## Toxic Blame Games

Blame games are a toxic trademark of narcissistic behavior, for narcs never realize their own mistakes and faults and quickly cover them up by deflecting and blaming others. If a project goes wrong because of their mistakes or carelessness, they will have no trouble or remorse blaming everything on you.

## Exploiting Weaknesses & Vulnerabilities

Narcissists have a meticulous and dedicated process of getting to know their victims and identifying their weak points and vulnerabilities. They take their time to help you open up to them and share your weaknesses and issues with immense comfort. Once the sharing process is over and the narcissist has ample leverage to exploit you, you will find the tables turning at the speed of lightning.

Before you know it, the narcissist will use your weak spots and vulnerabilities to exploit you into submission to their will and whims.

## Active Attempts to Sabotage Your Career

Suppose a narcissist sees you as a competitor or envies your success. In that case, they will do everything in their power to get you demoted, fired, or sabotage your career in every which way. They simply cannot help it. Now, this can prove alarming and disturbing when the narc is your boss or a superior who holds power and influence to sabotage your career. A narcissist will go above and beyond with their attempts to get you fired or get you into some sort of trouble that results in utter humiliation.

## Lying to Succeed

Narcissists lie very comfortably and confidently and do not feel any pangs of remorse while doing so. It's very common for a narcissistic coworker or boss to lie to get ahead and enjoy more recognition and applause.

## Striving to Be the BEST

Being the best at everything is a life goal for a narcissist, and naturally, this goal plays out at work more than it does in other life settings. Narcissists are constantly competing to be the best, and they are competing with everyone, not just you. Unfortunately, they don't allow fair competition based on hard work and dedication. Instead, narcissists compete with manipulative exploitation, and other tactics driven by their toxic and negative energies.

## Active Gossipmongers

Narcissists love to gossip, and they gossip with a carefully laid out strategy. First, they plan and plot to gain access to your secrets, weaknesses, and trigger points, and then they spread gossip about you. At times, this malicious gossip stems from fabrications and lies. It can cast a negative and unattractive light on you in your workplace. Confronting a narcissist is extremely hard because they will flat-out deny all accusations.

## Coercion to Commit Unethical Acts

Narcissist bosses and coworkers are notorious for putting others in a difficult position, challenging their values and moral beliefs. Narcs will pressure you into committing unethical acts, which could be anything from hurting, abusing, or humiliating another coworker, cheating a client, embezzling funds, or anything that burdens your conscience.

## Overpowering Jealousy

Narcs are brimming with jealousy, and their competitive streak always gets the best of them. They are incapable of feeling happy and proud of others, be it their family, children, or friends. Narcs are jealous of all those who succeed around them because in their minds, only they reserve the appropriate right to success, power, and glory. So, they will be jealous of your accomplishments and successes instead of congratulating you. Even if they congratulate you, it will be forced and only for the sake of appearances.

## Unwillingness to Be Questioned

Narcissists in a workplace refuse to be questioned by their subordinates and juniors in any form or manner. They see questioning as an insult to their brilliance and genius. They will not acknowledge someone's intellect or ability to help them correct their mistakes or add value to a project with constructive feedback. Narc bosses want to shout out commands, and they accept completion without any questions or criticism. Narcissists regard questioning as an act of challenging their authority, and they don't take this kindly. Questioning or challenging a narcissist will only encourage them to take up a vendetta against you. You definitely don't want that because they can get very committed and devoted to bringing you down and sabotaging your career.

## Demanding Undying Fealty, Admiration & Applause

Have you ever noticed how your narc boss, manager, or coworker moves around with an entourage of flying monkeys, fueling their ego with endless adoration, praise, admiration, and applause? It's common for narcs to surround themselves with people willing to pledge their undying loyalty and shower them with endless praise and adoration. Building a balanced relationship with a narcissist in the workplace is exceedingly challenging because they will demand your loyalty, admiration, and praise.

They will never be satisfied by what you give, no matter how ardently you admire and respect them. It's a vicious trap for everything you do or say just won't be enough for the narc to overcome their insecurities and return the favor.

## Autocratic Leadership Style

In the workplace, narcissists operate a lot like dictators and autocrats who want to seize power and control and demand total obedience. They are not feedback-oriented leaders, and they do not wish to engage in any conversation that involves solving problems and bringing changes. They do not associate any value with the opinions of others, and they are virtually incapable of listening to and incorporating feedback. They simply want to give orders and expect their orders to be followed verbatim.

Narcissists are not team players, and they don't care about the needs and values of other employees in the organization. It's very natural for a narcissist boss or manager to say, "So what if you have to visit your mother after her surgery; work and deadlines are more important." They don't care about the struggles employees or team members are facing in their personal lives. They don't care much about their employees' performance and professional growth either; they simply want to make life difficult for those who do not obey them in manners they wish to be obeyed. They have an overly autocratic and authoritative leadership style. Narcs also tend to make unilateral decisions without involving or discussing with other stakeholders.

## Delusions of Grandeur

Narcissists have an inflated sense of superiority that stems from their heightened delusions of grandeur. They want you to worship the floor they walk on because, in their minds, they possess such awe-inspiring brilliance and fantasized talents that make them worthy of endless applause and adoration. As a result, they are brimming with arrogance to the core, perpetually caught up in self-admiration and fawning over their own fantasized expertise and importance.

They are very focused and conscious about their self-image and public image. Narcs want everyone to act and think in a manner that elevates their public standing and reputation. As your boss, a narcissist will plan out every aspect of your day so you can work towards making them look good, perfect, and successful.

## The Pursuit of Power

Narcissists are obsessed with power, which makes sense how they manage to climb high up the corporate ladder, landing themselves in posh corporate settings and high-rise offices. They pursue power with a fierce vengeance and an unyielding passion. Not all people with narcissistic tendencies manage to actualize the power they crave, but for the ones who do, their thirst for power never ceases.

Narcissists in the workplace can be easily spotted by their demands and pursuit of extraordinary positional and personal power. They want their influence to be all-encompassing, enveloping everyone and everything in its tight-fisted claws. Thus, as corporate climbers, narcissists plot and scheme to spend most of their time with change-makers, power players, and high-status bigwigs in the organization. They are capable of respecting people they feel are their equals in terms of brilliance, genius, and success, but this respect only lasts until their competitive and envious streak kicks in.

A narcissist boss or manager wouldn't shy away from using the dirtiest tactic in the corporate playbook to coerce, cajole, and bully subordinates into submission. They utilize all tactics, from fear and guilt to shame, manipulation, and the threat of punishment, to ensure control and compliance. To them, you're just a meaning-less pawn on their chessboard, and only their strategy and gameplay can give your life purpose and meaning.

## COPING WITH A NARCISSISTIC BOSS OR A COLLEAGUE

Now that you know what signs to look out for in your professional environment, let's dive into ways to both productively work while protecting yourself from work-place narcissists. The following strategies will come in handy as you seek to further your career while main-taining calm while in the proximity of a narcissist. It can be intimidating especially in the case of a narcissist manager or boss, but if you are able to commit to some basic guidelines, you may find yourself in a safer and more predictable situation. In an article from Sarkis (2017), several strategies to maintain workplace sanity include:

## Emphasize the Need for Written Communication

When dealing with a narcissist, it's essential to emphasize the need for written communication. Narcissists have a habit of deflecting and denying. Having documentation in the form of emails or written notes can prove helpful in building a solid case. Emails directly sent by the narcissists or minutes of your meetings and interactions with them will help you thwart their attempts to sabotage your career. Be sure to review all your notes on their instructions to double-check for accuracy, and always maintain documentation and minutes so you can repeat their exact quotes verbatim with evidence in the form of paperwork or a voice recording. Should you ever feel the need to file an official Human Resources complaint or consult an attorney, all this evidence will help you establish solid grounds for legal proceedings.

## Steer Clear of Arguments & Fights

Getting into a fight with a narcissist is an utter waste of one's energy, be it a petty argument or a full-blown corporate rivalry. Narcissists actively seek drama, competition, hostility, and rivalries to keep themselves entertained with an outlet for their negativity. Don't become that outlet, and don't encourage them to find crafty tricks to ruin your career or demote you.

It may seem like I'm encouraging you to become a passive person. I'm not. I'm just trying to explain that avoiding fights is because narcissists always attack their targets below the belt by exposing their weaknesses and high-lighting their insecurities and secrets in painfully cruel ways. For instance, if you're constantly gushing over your little ones and feel sensitive about their needs, a narcissist is likely to gossip about your parenting style or your fail-ures as a spouse after you've experienced a messy divorce.

Avoiding fights is essential because a narcissist won't hesi-tate to push all kinds of buttons to encourage you to explode and act in ways that are extremely unlike you. So don't give them the satisfaction of an outburst, a debate, or any kind of conflict. Instead, dull their energies by walking away with a pleasant smile on your face. Witnessing their frustration at your calm demeanor is much more exciting than a cerebral debate with a narc.

### Don't Take It Personally

It's essential to regard your interactions or struggles with a narcissist as an unfortunate life event and avoid taking it personally. Keep in mind that narcissists are insecure and unwell. Most importantly, they are incapable of processing their and others' emotions. They choose their victims after being triggered by jealousy, competitiveness, or feeling challenged by someone's success and talents. Therefore, they are most likely to prey on successful, focused, performance-oriented people with a close-knit circle of friends to support them at work.

It's not personal. A narcissist hates nothing more than the idea of someone else claiming their trophy of excellence, perfection, and being the best. They don't want anyone to look or be perceived as their superior. So, their actions towards you have nothing to do with you and everything to do with their insecurities, vulnerabilities, and envious streak.

## Avoid Sharing Your Opinions & Secrets

Whatever you do, don't ever share personal information, secrets, and opinions with a narcissist. Now, this one is hardball because initially, they come off as very kind, considerate, and charming people, and you feel comfortable opening up to them. A classic narcissist would set the trap by asking, "So, what do you think about working with (a colleague)? Is he a good person?" If you manage to fall for this trap, they will twist and turn your answer into a grossly exaggerated version of the truth and use it to spread lies and gossip about you.

Remember, the narcissist embodies the traits of a quintessential emotional vampire. I know we agreed to avoid demonizing people for their mental condition. Still, this reference is necessary to explain how they prey on their victims by using their senses to push and probe until they've succeeded in hitting the rough spot.

Sharing any information about your personal relationships, be it about your parents, siblings, spouse, boyfriend, or children, will be added to their arsenal of weapons to use against you. That's just how they operate, and there's nothing you can do about it except being vigilant about the information you share with them. It is highly recommended that all dialogue and interactions are kept on a strictly professional level. Avoid any commentary or divulging of social or personal information.

## Keep a Witness Close By

Having a witness truly helps, especially if you feel heavily targeted and preyed upon by a narc boss. If your narcissist coworker or manager requests a private audience, consider having a witness around to lighten the situation. The witness will also help you provide evidence for your version of events should the narcissist attempt to lie about your meeting or interactions.

## Reduce Your Interaction

Reducing your interactions and shortening your conversations with narcissists is the best trick to stay off their radar. Don't engage with them. Instead, learn from the experiences of other coworkers who got the brunt of their narcissistic rage. Practice the grey rock method so you can be a dull and uninteresting target for their crafty schemes and clever strategies.

## Understanding Your Legal Rights

It's not uncommon for a narcissist to push you beyond your limits, causing grave psychological or even physical harm. Their envy, rage, and vengeance know no bounds, and they are likely to commit illegal acts. Understanding your legal rights as an employee is essential, especially if the narc is your manager, boss, or senior executive. According to employee rights in the United States, employees can start legal proceedings in cases of workplace bullying, harassment, or discrimination for their race, religion, sexual orientation, gender identity, pregnancy, or other reasons. You can also sue your employer for intolerable working conditions that caused you severe mental and physical stress, forcing you to quit.

## Don't Criticize or Challenge Them

Challenging, criticizing, or disagreeing with a narcissist will put you on their radar quicker than in the blink of an eye. Keep in mind that their fragile and vulnerable self-esteem cannot take the blow of your criticism; regardless of how constructive or carefully concocted it is, they will end up feeling devastated and furious. Don't discuss the impact of their decisions with them, no matter how adversely it impacts you, your team, or the organization. Instead, focus more on what you can do to come out as a productive and determined professional.

**Boost Their Ego**

I don't usually encourage people to indulge in false praise or use flattery as a tool to win support, but when dealing with a narcissist, it's a trick that can work wonders (Tabaka, 2017). It may make you feel exploitative, but flatter and praise can give you enormous power over them. Praising them and boosting their ego will empower you with the control to get into their head and make them amiable enough to collaborate productively. Praising their abilities and talents will help you ensure timely completion without much conflict. However, be prepared for them to take all the credit for the work.

**Watch Out for the Gaslighting!**

Narcissists are masters at making you doubt your talents, qualities, and capabilities, encouraging you to find faults in yourself (*How to Deal With a Narcissist at Work*, n.d.). This exploitative and manipulative strategy is popularly known as gaslighting, and it works like a lethal poison.

Some common gaslighting tactics include:

- Making you question your memory or recollection of events.
- Changing the subject during a pressing discussion.
- Labeling your issues and concerns as "small" or "meaningless."
- Outright denying their narcissist rage and selfish behaviors.

When dealing with a narcissist, it's essential to trust your instincts and rely on your version of reality. Because if you give in to their gaslighting attempts, they will transform you from victim to villain before you know it. Again, having evidence in the form of recordings, instructions or emails will help you focus the discussion on your version of reality and prevent them from misleading or distorting facts.

**Never Confront Them**

Confronting a narcissist is the worst thing you can do because it will validate that all their schemes and plotting to sabotage your achievements are working. Confronting a narc will only confirm that their attacks hit the target and succeeded in triggering you and summoning your anger and frustration. Once you lose control, the narcissist will turn the tables and play the most convincing and tragedy-stricken victim. Don't let their Oscar-worthy performances paint you as the villain.

Instead of confronting the narc directly, focus on collecting evidence and documenting everything so you can present your case with a solid argument should the need arise for legal proceedings.

**Accept That Change Is Unlikely**

Accepting that a narcissist will never change, not until they make an active and intentional effort, will help you move through their negativity and drama without being affected in the slightest. This simple belief will help you deal with their tantrums and negativity in a positive manner, making it easier to cope with the toxic environment at work.

If you can't ignore them, detach yourself or escape the trauma and negativity they are adding to your life, and consider exploring other work opportunities to eliminate the strain on your emotional and mental well-being.

# 6

# CO-PARENTING WITH A
# NARCISSIST

There's nothing more maddening and complicated than staying tied to a narcissist because of your children. Even after taking the big plunge and distancing yourself, it's incredibly challenging to maintain contact as a co-parent. The first thing to understand and embrace is that you cannot avoid interaction until your children are grown adults (Smith, 2021). Till then, your narcissist co-parent will remain an annoying and frustrating fixture in your life and those of your children. Now, you cannot help your ex realize their mistakes or make them aware of their narcissistic behavior. Still, you can tackle their complexities and attacks with a collaborative, positive, and firm attitude.

It's a scary process and coming from someone who has lived through this struggle, it truly helps to ground yourself in positivity and a collaborative mindset. I remember the custody swap that ensued during our divorce battle. I remember feeling extremely uncomfortable being alone in his presence after our separation, so I often requested my best friend to accompany me while dropping off and picking up my sons. I asked her to accompany me to feel physically safe and mentally secure. But he truly surprised me, even after living with him and experiencing his narcissistic behavior, by twisting the reality around. He told his attorney that I was "intimidating and bullying him with my cadre." The cadre being my best friend and her eight-year-old daughter.

It's hard, and it won't get easier until you try to make it easier with a straightforward transactional system of dealing with your narcissistic ex. Let's dive into the challenges of co-parenting with a narcissist and equip you with some powerful strategies to navigate the toxicity and negativity of this harrowing ordeal.

## THE CHALLENGES OF CO-PARENTING WITH A NARCISSIST

Co-parenting with a narcissist comes with a plethora of overwhelming challenges, but on the bright side, cooperative thinking can help you overcome anything and everything. Even agreeable and healthy parents struggle to manage their time and agree on all the stipulations and terms of a custody agreement. However, with a narcissist, it's hard to get them to agree to anything that facilitates your life.

So, the pressure to cooperate and be amicable will fall on you. With your attitude, firmness, and cooperative thinking, you can smoothen out the situation and make it more bearable for all parties, particularly yourself and your children. As we dive deeper into this chapter, I want you to keep in mind that narcissists are incapable of cooperating and facilitating others. Embracing this reality will make the ordeal less burdensome and challenging (Marcin, 2020).

## Turning Your Kids against You

It's pertinent to note that your narcissistic ex will struggle to get over the fact that you had the courage and, in their minds, the audacity to give up and walk out on them. Your courage and resilience to leave them will have them fuming in anger, fury, and most alarmingly, the fire of vengeance. They will want to hurt you and attack you in ways that make them the victim and paint you the villain, and for this purpose, they will use your children as pawns in their dirty game.

The entire co-parenting situation serves the purpose of allowing the children open access to both parents, but in most cases, it ends up embroiling the kids in a war between their parents. You may not do anything to trigger or fuel this war and pollute the minds of your little ones with negativity against their parent, but don't expect your narcissistic ex to return the favor.

A narcissist co-parent will do everything in their power to use your kids against you and pollute their minds with unimaginable debris. Divorce is a very challenging and complex turmoil for children. Because they don't understand the dynamics of adult relationships and behaviors, they often struggle to pick sides and blame someone. Your narcissistic co-parent can paint you as the culprit who shattered the family and broke up a happy home.

Being prepared will help you steer your children in the right direction with counseling efforts and connecting with their emotional well-being.

### Refusing to Agree with the Arrangements

It's very natural for a narcissist co-parent to deflect and divert from the arrangement and create disturbances to force you into arguments and fights with them. They will, time and again, violate the agreed arrangements, disrupt your schedule and try to inconvenience you in more ways than one.

They will purposefully interfere with your child's routine and appointments or misplace their belongings. In some cases, they can even refuse to return certain belongings, creating disturbances and inconveniences.

### Acting Disagreeable & Disruptive

Despite all the trauma and the abuse, you've agreed to the co-parenting arrangement for the well-being and health of your children. Keep in mind that the narcissist will not regard the co-parenting situation from this perspective.

Instead, the narcissistic co-parent will see it as an insult to their brilliance and an attack on their superiority. And they will not waste a single opportunity to express their discontentment and anger with narcissistic outbursts and their typical rage.

Don't expect your narcissistic co-parent to act pleasant or agreeable for the sake of your children. They are simply incapable of doing things selflessly for others. Being prepared for their problematic nature and troublemaking attitude will help you avoid surprises and focus on grounding your positive energies.

## HOW TO DEAL WITH THE CHALLENGES OF CO-PARENTING WITH A NARCISSIST

Have you noticed a common and familiar pattern in all the challenges I've just walked you through? These challenges reveal a common theme: the narcissist's desire and the struggle for control and domination.

Dealing with this relentless struggle for power and control is endlessly and overwhelmingly frustrating. Suppose you sense any form of emotional or physical abuse. In that case, you have solid grounds to keep your children away from your narc ex. However, doing everything in your power and within reason to keep both parents in a child's life is the healthiest, most effective decision you can make. Your children will forever applaud your efforts and patience in giving them the most normal childhood you could, given the circumstances.

Let's look at some strategies and techniques to help you deal with a narcissistic co-parent effectively and firmly (Marcin, 2020).

**A Legal Co-Parenting Plan**

Do not embark on a co-parenting journey with your narcissistic ex without a legal parenting plan to provide both parents with a roadmap. Without a written legal agreement, you cannot expect a narcissist to seize their attempts to take control and dominate the situation. Having a legal custody agreement and parenting plan will protect you from your ex's manipulative tactics and unreasonable demands.

You see, legal agreements involve third-party actors, such as law enforcement and attorneys, to help you formally enforce the stipulations of the agreement and prevent violations. The plan must include everything, from visitation schedules and durations of holidays and everyday routine, alongside a breakdown of costs and expenses. It's crucial to work closely with your attorney while drafting a custody agreement to ensure it covers all the grey areas and vulnerabilities your ex is likely to use against you. The legal costs may add up, but this contract will give you the peace of mind of not having to argue and fight over every little thing while co-parenting with a narcissist.

**Handling Custody Swaps Safely**

Custody swaps can easily become a point of contention. Following a few ground rules pertaining to these potentially confrontational exchanges will help immensely. The following guidelines are a few simple ideas to encourage safe custody swaps (HG.org, n.d.):

1. Swap kids on neutral territory (e.g., police station, if necessary).
2. Understand your rights about custody within an established court order.
3. Be sure to document each swap.
4. Do not engage in conversation about pending legal issues.
5. Create a no-contact swap where a neutral and safe third party accepts and releases the child to the co-parent.

## Rely on Legal Services & Processes

Do you have an overwhelmingly difficult time with the manipulative tactics of your narcissistic co-parent? Instead of engaging with the narcissist, it's wiser to turn to courts and seek help through a legal process. In cases of extreme and unavoidable conflict, the court can assign a parent coordinator to help with communication and scheduling. Parent coordinators are certified and trained professionals equipped with the right tools and authority to handle such cases. Besides, the support and freedom you will get from having an independent and unbiased third-party coordinator are genuinely priceless. You and the children will find it significantly easier to bring your narcissistic ex to comply with the system created by the legal co-parenting plan. Besides, a narcissist is likely to be the best version of themselves around a third-party evaluator as they wouldn't dare ruin their shining image with outbursts and rage.

In cases of custody disputes with a narcissistic ex, it's common for victims to seek the court's assistance in the appointment of a Guardian ad Litem (GAL) to secure the legal interests of their child. The GAL acts as a supporter, advocate, and mediator. You can rely on their assistance in times of distress and confusion.

## Assert Your Boundaries with Firmness

Once you've taken the giant leap of eliminating the narcissist from your life, you no longer have to tip-toe around them, scared of unleashing the narcissistic rage. Now, you can assert your boundaries with more firmness and resilience, and they will feel threatened by the consequences of pushing you too far. Avoid getting into arguments and fights, but don't let the fear of a fight or disagreement compel you to repeal your boundaries and relax with firmness.

## Become an Empathetic & Compassionate Parent

There may be times when your children will question your version of events and blame you for their broken home, fueled by the negativity and toxic brainwashing of a narcissistic ex. Such moments can be earth-shattering for a victim of narcissistic abuse. Still, it's essential to rein in your emotions and be as empathetic as possible. Try to put yourself in the minds of your little ones and try to understand that their cognitive capabilities cannot process the enormity of the lies they have been exposed to by their narcissistic parent.

Deal with their outbursts, sadness, and grief with compassion, and help them recover and grow into healthy and kind adults. As children mature, they will come to see the truth and realize on their own which parent is the healthy one when they are dealt with this level of care.

## Don't Badmouth Your Co-Parent

Here's another struggle that most victims experience and usually end up succumbing to the pressure and waves of hate boiling inside them. It's hard to keep yourself from talking about and rationalizing the trauma you have suffered but doing it in front of the children will only corrupt and corrode their innocence.

Children find solace and strength in believing that their parents are good people and models they can look up to for guidance and advice. Don't shatter that mental model by speaking ill of the other parent in front of your children. In most cases, children always end up getting burned and challenged by their narcissistic parent, so you won't need to explain much of the situation as leaving the raging and demanding parent will be as much of an escape for them as it is for you.

## Escape Emotionally-Charged Conversations

Getting into emotional arguments and conversations charged with sentiments that make you vulnerable will make you feel just that—overwhelmed and vulnerable. Avoid these conversations at all costs and find peace and relaxation in the fact that your life is now free of all chaos and disturbance. Revel in this newfound existence, prioritize your peace, and preserve your mental energies by avoiding emotionally charged arguments.

## Get Ready to Combat Challenges

Are you relying on your narcissistic co-parent to keep up with their end of the bargain? If yes, then you're going to be bitterly and sorely disappointed. In contrast, if you're mentally prepared for challenges and difficulties, you'll have a much easier time countering these obstacles.

You see, a narcissistic co-parent will do everything in their power to win back control and power, and craft new strategies and plots to corner and attack you. Don't let that happen. If they've missed an appointment, reschedule it again and take charge of the responsibility yourself. If they failed to attend a basketball game that meant the world to your child, don't engage or confront them. Instead, find ways to soothe the situation and help your child process the disappointment positively. Focus and prioritize your child and their needs as you take the high road and interact with the narcissistic co-parent in a manner that doesn't stoop to their level.

## Collect Evidence at All Times

Now, while you shouldn't confront or challenge your narcissistic co-parent, meticulously collecting evidence of their misbehavior, outbursts, and violations of the legal agreement will prove immensely beneficial. As a healthy and mindful person, it's hard to plan and scheme to collect evidence against someone. Mostly, we find ourselves shocked and alarmed by their narcissistic behaviors. At that moment, it's almost like we've frozen with the shock of their unpredictably rash behavior, unable to grasp our phones and make a recording. It's only later when we look back at events that we lament ourselves for not acting fast enough to record everything they did or said.

That's a mistake that you should never make after leaving and embarking on a co-parenting situation. Be sure to document everything they say, especially their violations and behavior so that you can challenge and confront your narcissistic co-parent through the legal system.

## Find a Counselor

Nothing good ever comes out of acting brave and drowning your vulnerabilities, trauma, and grief with concern for your children. Considering counseling and therapy for yourself and the children will do your family a world of good. Living with a narcissist and surviving the ordeal shouldn't make you feel weak and vulnerable. In fact, it should brim you with the power of the realization that you're a survivor who survived against insurmountable odds.

Counseling and therapy will help you and the kids process the bitter emotions and the complex trauma triggered by the narcissistic traits. Unraveling the trauma won't be easy, but it will make you lighter, happier, and more productive. Most importantly, it will help you cleanse out the bitterness and dig deeper to understand and process everything you've suffered all these years. It's essential to consider therapy for the children to help them process and overcome the negative emotions of their adverse childhood experiences.

## Don't Engage in Conflict

Realizing that a narcissist's attacks stem from their own insecurities and sensitivity to criticism will help you win half the battle long before getting up to fight. And as this realization deepens, you will have abandoned the need to fight altogether. Their insecurities, vulnerabilities, rage, and inflated ego are on them—not you. So let them marinate in all that negativity, and don't let it inch near your mind.

Remind yourself that the conflict doesn't stem from getting stuck in traffic and arriving a few minutes later than the scheduled time, or your firm refusal to let your kids stay over on a school night. The conflict stems from their exaggerated sense of superiority and their audacity to think they can continue dominating and overpowering you. Instead of responding to their hate and negativity, ground your energies on staying cool and reveling in your calm state of mind. In the long run, your children will remember the parent who shouted and the parent who stayed calm in the face of a storm, and this alone will strengthen your relationship with them.

## Explore Parallel Parenting

When co-parenting arrangements don't seem to work, parallel parenting presents a viable solution. It's an arrangement that doesn't require you to maintain any contact with your ex whatsoever. Parallel parenting allows both parents to parent their child in whichever way they seem fit when the child is in their custody. You won't have to attend parent-teacher conferences and school events quivering in fear of being embarrassed by your narcissistic ex and his infamous tantrums.

Parallel parenting allows you to avoid all communication until it's essential to communicate. It allows children to escape the trauma and stress of seeing their parents fight, malign, and abuse one another. However, do you trust your narcissistic ex enough to entrust your children into their care? In most cases, narcissists have a very damaging and toxic impact on their kids, and malignant narcs aren't safe to be around.

## Prioritize Your Children above All Else

It's essential to prioritize the well-being and comfort of your child above all else. The narcissistic co-parent has rights, as a parent, but do they deserve close access to your child? Most importantly, does your child feel safe, loved, and accepted by your narc ex?

Suppose your child is quivering with fear and over-whelming stress at the thought of meeting the co-parent after a prolonged break. Would you encourage them to put aside their fear and comply with the legal process?

You may want the narcissistic co-parent to remain a figure in your children's lives, but is it genuinely worth endangering the mental and physical well-being of your child? If the child is visibly uncomfortable and distressed, it's essential to prioritize counseling to help them process these difficult emotions. You must also seek legal help to reduce or limit interactions with the co-parent until your child is ready and willing to initiate contact again. If you suspect that your child is in a dangerous situation with your co-parent, it is advisable to seek a psychological evaluation. If the evaluation concludes that your co-parent is considered a danger to your child, documentation from such an evaluation will strengthen your case for decreased custody time with the narcissist.

## Communicate with Firm Rules

Setting ground rules to define the communication between you and your ex will help you escape the horridly traumatic outbursts and manipulative text messages that leave you reeling with pain and frustration.

How accessible are you for your narcissistic ex? Can they pick up the phone, dial your number and ruin your peace whenever they like? Or are there some ground rules around the timing and matters they can disturb you for or communicate with you? Setting some firm rules will help you enjoy mental peace and create an impregnable wall around you—a wall they cannot climb or dismantle even with their most concentrated and dedicated efforts.

## Set Up Consistent Call Times with the Children

As children are juggled between each co-parent, the need for children to communicate should be carefully coordinated. There will likely be moments where the narcissistic co-parent will attempt to contact your child against your wishes (*Co-Parenting With a Narcissist: How to Make It Work*, n.d.). The best remedy for this issue is to establish set times that the co-parent can contact the child. Having specific times to work within will enable fair communication between the narcissistic parent while protecting yourself from the accusation of parental alienation.

## Don't Drag Your Child into the Mess

The narcissistic abuse and co-parenting model has already created unbelievable confusion and trauma in your children's minds. They are struggling to understand the issues separating the two most important adults in their lives and the breaking of their family. Don't overload them with more trauma, confusion, and conflicting emotions.

Naturally, your narcissistic co-parent is not healthy enough to make such a mindful decision. In contrast, they will do everything in their power to drag the children into the mess and use them as pawns against you. You must not do the same and channel your power from positivity. Instead of indulging in the smear campaign and blame game, teach your children compassion and help them empathize and rebuild their confidence.

## Work within Your Limits

As you co-parent with a narcissist, you will soon learn that you will be limited by your actions. You are working with a person who will use any emotion from you to their advantage. The sooner you realize that it is for the best that you accept you are unable to impact their behavior and that you only have control over your own actions, the better.

## Set a Powerful Precedent

A narcissist is utterly clueless when it comes to working amicably and cooperatively because their inflated ego always gets in the way. Still, you can set the tone of the relationship by establishing a powerful precedent. The idea is to lead by example and use your cooperative behavior and positive attitude to set an inspiring precedent for the narcissist and your children.

While it's futile to expect the narcissist to feel inspired and change into a cooperative person overnight, they will catch up with the program and eventually understand that coercion no longer works in their relationship with you. But you must focus on setting this precedent more for your children than for the narcissist because someone must show them the human face of kindness, empathy, compassion, generosity, care, and cooperation.

Their narcissistic parent won't show them the art of emulating these qualities, so the responsibility falls entirely on you. Your child's future relationships will depend on how they see us treating others—even those who are unkind to us.

## Embrace Our Family Wizard/TalkingParents

A third-party calendar system, such as Our Family Wizard, can genuinely work wonders at making co-parenting easier and reducing the need to communicate too often. It will help devise an easily manageable schedule that covers all co-parenting duties and eliminates the need for unnecessary discussions. The system comes with a message board to regulate all your communications without the need for in-person or even over-the-phone contact. It will streamline all events and activities and offers a journal feature for any notes or instructions you may want to add to help the co-parent keep your children safe and prepared for their basketball games, sleep time rituals, and other specifics. Most amazingly, this calendar system comes with an info bank and an expense log to track all the co-parenting expenses and reduce the risk of arguments and conflicts over financial matters.

As an alternative, TalkingParents is a similar communication system and includes a feature where private phone conversations between co-parents can be recorded. Transcripts to these conversations are available for future reference.

## Avoid Sharing Personal Information

Are you gradually finding your way back to the dating field, and trying to open yourself up for romantic advances with healthy and positive people? Or perhaps, you're planning to reclaim your confidence by starting a new business venture, learning a new skill, or going back to school. No matter what you plan and do, don't share any personal goals, plans and information with your narcissistic ex.

Your life goals, plans, and achievements will only trigger their narcissistic rage, envy, and competitiveness, encouraging the narcissist to plot and scheme, and eventually cause you discomfort or pain. Remember, with your children shuffling between both parents; the narcissist still has the leverage to hurt you. They don't care if the children end up being collateral damage in the fight to satisfy and stroke their ego. But you must be careful and avoid triggering their narcissistic tendencies by sharing news of personal growth and wellness.

## Protect Yourself

When co-parenting with a narcissist, it is undoubtedly extremely frustrating. In these co-parenting situations, there will be the need for communication and communication must be minimized to solely discussions about the children. However, narcissists may seize these opportunities to hurt, intimidate, or threaten you. To avoid unnecessary stress, it is advisable to be active in seeking protection for yourself. Take measures to avoid being further hurt by your narcissist by employing tactics such as having a third party (perhaps a close friend) read emails or texts and distill it down to only what is necessary for you to know. This will filter out any negative and unnecessary commentary from your narc.

I hope you have enjoyed *Dealing with the Unavoidable Narcissist in Your Life* so far. Before we wrap it up with my final words, I would be incredibly thankful if you would leave a brief review – even if it's just a few sentences.

Thank you!

# CONCLUSION

No one can remain unhinged and balanced in the face of targeted coercive attempts to usurp your control and strip you of your self-esteem. Narcissistic abuse comes in a series of ugly faces, constantly ricocheting between intermittent reward if you do the narc's bidding and torturous punishment if you fail to please the unpleasable. Satisfying a narcissist is the most futile and fruitless of endeavors. It leads to a vicious cycle of punishment and reward and brainwashing tactics that leave you feeling powerless, vulnerable, and unbelievably hurt. Ending this vicious cycle is genuinely the best way to preserve your sanity, emotional well-being, life quality, and self-esteem.

Before you finish reading this book and move forward in your life, guided by its support and knowledge, I want you to embrace and respect yourself as a true survivor. You are a survivor through and through, and I am incredibly proud of you for taking the initiative of understanding this complex condition and making a healthy choice to dismantle the roots of trauma in your life.

Dealing with an unempathetic person who fails to acknowledge and respect you as a person, treating you with haughty disdain, looking down at you like a minuscule insect, and trampling over your emotions is never easy. The best way to deal with such people is by not dealing with them at all. Remember the grey rock method? Becoming an unresponsive, dull, and insignificant grey rock will help you escape the attention of a narcissist. However, this method alone isn't enough when dealing with a close family member who doesn't seem to get dissuaded by your firmness and boundaries.

Here's a little recap of the strategies we've discussed:

- Acknowledging the condition: narcissistic personality disorder (NPD).
- Refusal to engage with disrespectful behavior and toxic attitudes.
- Distancing yourself from narcissistic abuse.
- Understanding that you're not the culprit and stop taking their behavior personally.
- Find support through family and friends.
- Engage a therapist experienced with narcissism to cope with the trauma and abuse.
- Being compassionate with yourself, children, and other loved ones caught up in between.
- Using your empathy, kindness, and compassion as

strengths as opposed to weaknesses to be exploited.

The power to break free from the trauma and the struggle lies within you. You've been ignoring it to give your best to your relationship. Always remember that appeasing a narcissist can only go so far. Their hunger for your love, selfless generosity, and loyal obedience will only increase. End this vicious cycle now by pouring all that love and care into nurturing yourself, and when you do, you will be surprised to find you are more than you ever imagined yourself to be!

If you would like additional support
as you deal with the narcissist in your life,
we'd love to have you join our Facebook group:
The Road to Narcissistic Abuse Recovery

Don't forget to grab your free gift!
*Your 7 Step Journey to Narcissistic Abuse Recovery*

*www.TrilliumSage.com*

# REFERENCES

Bagai, S. (n.d.). *Dealing with narcissistic personality disorder in the Workplace.* Www.Crowdstaffing.Com. Retrieved July 13, 2021, from https://www.crowdstaffing.com/blog/ dealing-with-narcissistic-personality-disorder-in-the-workplace-2.

Brazier, Y. (2020, September 29). *All about narcissistic personality disorder.* Www.Medicalnewstoday.Com. https://www.medicalnewstoday.com/articles/ 9741#symptoms.

Caporuscio, J. (2021, February 1). *What is the grey rock method?* Www.Medicalnewstoday.Com. https://www. medicalnewstoday.com/articles/grey-rock#summary.

Caprino, K. (2016, July 9). *How Being Raised By A Narcissist Damages Your Life And Self-Esteem.* Www.Forbes.Com.

https://www.insider.com/sibling-dynamics-behaviors-narcissistic-families-2019-7.

Cherry, K. (2020, November 20). *What Is narcissistic personality disorder (NPD)?* Www.Verywellmind.Com. https://www.verywellmind.com/what-is-narcissistic-personality-disorder-2795446.

Cherry, K. (2021a, May 7). *What Is Cognitive Behavioral Therapy (CBT)?* Www.Verywellmind.Com. https://www.verywellmind.com/what-is-cognitive-behavior-therapy-2795747.

Cherry, K. (2021b, June 12). *What Is Psychotherapy?* Www.Verywellmind.Com. https://www.verywellmind.com/psychotherapy-4157172.

Clarke, J. (2020, July 27). *How to Recognize Someone With Covert Narcissism.* Www.Verywellmind.Com. https://www.verywellmind.com/understanding-the-covert-narcissist-4584587#overt-vs-covert.

*Co-Parenting With a Narcissist: How to Make It Work.* (n.d.). Www.2houses.Com. Retrieved July 14, 2021, from https://www.2houses.com/en/blog/co-parenting-with-a-narcissist-how-to-make-it-work.

Cunha, J. (2020, August 10). *What Are the Nine Traits of a Narcissist?* Www.Emedicinehealth.Com. https://www.emedicinehealth.com/what_are_the_nine_traits_of_a_narcissist/article_em.htm.

@dealwithnarcissist. (2020, February 12). *9 signs of a narcissistic sibling, family dynamics and how to deal with narcissistic siblings.* Www.Dealwithnarcissist.Com. https://www.dealwithnarcissist.com/narcissistic-siblings-about-signs-of-a-narcissistic-sibling-the-effect-they-have-and-how-to-deal-with-a-narcissistic-sibling/.

Dodgson, L. (2020, April 29). *The 5 most common themes in narcissistic families, from "flying monkeys" to the "needy sibling."* Www.Insider.Com. https://www.insider.com/sibling-dynamics-behaviors-narcissistic-families-2019-7.

Fjelstad, M. (2020, September 30). *15 Signs You're Dealing With A Narcissist.* Www.Mindbodygreen.Com. https://www.mindbodygreen.com/articles/14-signs-of-narcissism.

Franco, G. (n.d.). *How to Deal With a Narcissistic Mother.* Cbtpsychology.Com. Retrieved July 14, 2021, from https://cbtpsychology.com/narcissisticmother/.

Galperin, S. (n.d.). *How to Survive a Narcissistic Father.* Cbtpsychology.Com. Retrieved July 14, 2021, from https://cbtpsychology.com/survive-narcissistic-father/.

Glass, L. (2020, September 1). *Codependency & Narcissism: What's The Connection?* Www.Lovetopivot.Com. https://www.lovetopivot.com/difference-narcissism-codependency-attachment-style-intensive-retreat/.

Gould, W. (2020, December 8). *What Is Codependency?* Www.Verywellmind.Com. https://www.verywellmind.com/what-is-codependency-5072124.

Greenberg, E. (2021, February 13). *7 False Myths About narcissistic personality disorder.* Www.Psychologytoday.-Com. https://www.psychologytoday.com/us/blog/understanding-narcissism/202102/7-false-myths-about-narcissistic-personality-disorder.

Health Direct. (n.d.). *narcissistic personality disorder (NPD).* Www.Healthdirect.Gov.Au. Retrieved July 13, 2021, from https://www.healthdirect.gov.au/narcissistic-personality-disorder-npd.

HG.org. (n.d.). *Child Custody Exchange Safety.* Www.Hg.Org. Retrieved July 13, 2021, from https://www.hg.org/legal-articles/child-custody-exchange-safety-29599.

*How to Deal With a Narcissist at Work.* (n.d.). Www.Developgoodhabits.Com. Retrieved July 14, 2021, from https://www.developgoodhabits.com/how-to-deal-with-a-narcissist/#How_to_Deal_With_a_Narcissist_at_Work.

Inner Integration. (2016, October 24). *Gray Rock Technique — When You Have Kids With The Narcissist.* Www.Youtube.-Com. https://www.youtube.com/watch?v=e6n6r0kRtnw&list=PLDIP-IWPRMEzO4xgBIHqTF4PAypWNB2ms&index=12.

Kacel, E., Ennis, N., & Pereira, D. (2017). narcissistic personality disorder in Clinical Health Psychology Practice: Case Studies of Comorbid Psychological Distress and Life-Limiting Illness. *Behavioral Medicine, 43*(3), 156–164.

https://www.tandfonline.com/doi/full/10. 1080/08964289.2017.1301875.

Kritz, F. (2020, December 6). *What Is Narcissism? Symptoms, Causes, Diagnosis, Treatment, and Prevention.* Www.Everydayhealth.Com. https://www. everydayhealth.com/narcissism/.

Launder, A. (n.d.). *The Impact of Growing Up With A Narcissistic Parent.* Theawarenesscentre.Com. Retrieved July 14, 2021, from https://theawarenesscentre.com/narcissistic-parent/.

Luo, Y., Cai, H., & Song, H. (2014, April 2). *A Behavioral Genetic Study of Intrapersonal and Interpersonal Dimensions of Narcissism.* Www.Ncbi.Nlm.Nih.Gov. https://www. ncbi.nlm.nih.gov/pmc/articles/PMC3973692/.

Marcin, A. (2020, March 20). *Co-Parenting with a Narcissist: Tips for Making It Work.* Www.Healthline.Com. https:// www.healthline.com/health/parenting/co-parenting-with-a-narcissist#challenges.

Mayfield, E. (2020, November 30). *Why do narcissists attract codependents?* Www.Mindsettherapyonline.Com. https://www.mindsettherapyonline.com/blog/why-do-narcissists-attract-codependents.

Mental Health America. (n.d.). *Co-Dependency.* Mhanational.Org. Retrieved July 13, 2021, from https://www. mhanational.org/co-dependency.

Mitra, P., & Fluyau, D. (2021, May 18). *narcissistic personality disorder*. Www.Ncbi.Nlm.Nih.Gov. https://www.ncbi.nlm.nih.gov/books/NBK556001/.

*Narcissistic Brother and Sister Sibling Traits*. (n.d.). Narcissistabusesupport.Com. Retrieved July 14, 2021, from https://narcissistabusesupport.com/how-to-identify-narcissistic-siblings-narcissistic-brother-sister/.

O'Connell, B. (2021, February 23). *The Damage Done: Dealing with Narcissists in the Workplace*. Www.Shrm.Org. https://www.shrm.org/resourcesandtools/hr-topics/people-managers/pages/narcissism-and-managers-.aspx.

Plato's Stunt Double. (2020, July 16). *What is the difference between mobbing and bullying*. Flyingmonkeysdenied.Com. https://flyingmonkeysdenied.com/2015/12/01/what-is-the-difference-between-bullying-and-mobbing/.

Raypole, C. (2019, December 12). *Dealing With a Manipulative Person? Grey Rocking May Help*. Www.Healthline.Com. https://www.healthline.com/health/grey-rock#keep-in-touch-with-yourself.

Rosenberg, R. (2013, November 21). *The History of the Term, Codependency*. Psychcentral.Com. https://psychcentral.com/blog/human-magnets/2013/11/the-history-of-the-term-codependency#1.

Salters-Pedneault, K. (2020, April 1). *Understanding Psychotropic Drugs*. Www.Verywellmind.Com. https://www.verywellmind.com/psychotropic-drugs-425321.

Sarkis, S. (2017, January 18). *7 Ways to Cope With Narcissists at Work.* Www.Psychologytoday.Com. https://www.psychologytoday.com/us/blog/here-there-and-everywhere/201701/7-ways-cope-narcissists-work.

Saskia, S. (2016, January 11). *10 Tips for Co-Parenting with a Narcissist.* Www.Psychologytoday.Com. https://www.psychologytoday.com/us/blog/here-there-and-everywhere/201601/10-tips-co-parenting-narcissist.

Scott, E. (2020, December 17). *How to Identify a Malignant Narcissist.* Www.Verywellmind.Com. https://www.verywellmind.com/how-to-recognize-a-narcissist-4164528.

Smith, N. (2021, June 10). *Co-Parenting with a Narcissist: The Do's and Don'ts.* Www.Survivedivorce.Com. https://www.survivedivorce.com/co-parenting-narcissist.

Stinson, F., Dawson, D., Goldstein, R., Chou, S., Huang, B., Smith, S., Ruan, W., Pulay, A., Saha, T., Pickering, R., & Grant, B. (2008). https://www.ncbi.nlm.nih.gov/pmc/articles/PMC2669224/. *Prevalence, Correlates, Disability, and Comorbidity of DSM-IV narcissistic personality disorder: Results from the Wave 2 National Epidemiologic Survey on Alcohol and Related Conditions, 69*(7), 1033–1045. https://www.ncbi.nlm.nih.gov/pmc/articles/PMC2669224/.

Tabaka, M. (2017, January 23). *How to Deal With a Toxic Narcissist at Work.* Www.Inc.Com. https://www.inc.com/marla-tabaka/how-to-deal-with-a-toxic-narcissist-at-work.html.

The National Institute of Mental Health Information Resource Center. (n.d.). *Personality Disorders*. Www.N-imh.Nih.Gov. Retrieved July 14, 2021, from https://www.nimh.nih.gov/health/statistics/personality-disorders.

Thomas, N. (2021, January 5). *10 Signs of a Narcissistic Parent, & How to Deal With Them*. Www.Choosingtherapy.-Com. https://www.choosingtherapy.com/narcissistic-parent/.

Villines, Z. (2018, August 7). *Codependency and Narcissism May Have More in Common Than You Think*. Www.-Goodtherapy.Org. https://www.goodtherapy.org/blog/codependency-narcissism-may-have-more-in-common-than-you-think-0807187.

Whitbourne, S. (2016, January 5). *9 Myths about Narcissism Almost Everyone Believes*. Www.Psychologytoday.Com. https://www.psychologytoday.com/us/blog/fulfillment-any-age/201601/9-myths-about-narcissism-almost-everyone-believes.

Zajenkowski, M., Maciantowicz, O., Szymaniak, K., & Urban, P. (2018, August 28). *Vulnerable and Grandiose Narcissism Are Differentially Associated With Ability and Trait Emotional Intelligence*. Www.Frontiersin.Org. https://www.frontiersin.org/articles/10.3389/fpsyg.2018.01606/full.

# ABOUT THE AUTHOR

Sydney Koh was born in Singapore and raised in sunny Southern California. Having escaped her marriage of 15 years to a narcissist husband, she now seeks to empower others in their quest to regain their sense of self – transforming victims into survivors. She loves life with her three boisterous sons and German Shepherd, Yogi.

Made in the USA
Coppell, TX
10 January 2023

10895461R00109